"I've had the opportunity to see Ra̶n̶~~~~ple from addiction to a life fulfille̶~~~~ ~~~~ ̶ ̶ ̶ ̶ ̶is able to empower positive transformation in life's more difficult and complex problems with incredible clarity and accessibility. Contained in this book is profound truth about an abundant life for those willing to embrace it and put it into practice. Truly a transforming book for all."

—*Chris Williams*
Marriage and Family Therapist / Addiction and Trauma Specialist
Co-host, *New Life Live with Steve Arterburn*

"As a leader and teacher, Randal Smalls brings imagination, energy, and insight. He understands the journey and brings wisdom, clarity, and hope to this world through *Builders and Blockers of Life*. It will change an individual's direction if they purpose to apply it."

—*Joel Pagett*
Lead pastor, Reliance Community Church
Ontario, California

"Randal Smalls has shown the heart to guide me to the fruition of my vision of being happy, healthy, and free from addiction. He is a treasure—believing in me against all odds. I can't say enough about his wisdom and experience. Randal just "gets it," and I'm so blessed that he's been willing to share "it" with me. Now, as he shares it with the world through *Builders and Blockers of Life*, I have no doubt that everyone, especially those struggling in any way, can benefit from this book, filled with solutions for finding a better life."

—*El DeBarge*
Musician

"At Destiny House, our staff routinely deals with life and death crises in the lives of ladies who have been affected by serious trauma due to sexual abuse and sex trafficking. I believe that *Builders and Blockers of Life* is a critical tool that can be used as a catalyst of change to help them and others to come out of the darkness of addiction and into the bright light of self-awareness, freedom, and hope. Read this book—if not for yourself, for those who need the love of Jesus to open their eyes to the truth that they too can be set free to live lives of amazing destiny that they've always wanted."

—*Annie Lobert*
Author, *Fallen*
Founder of Hookers for Jesus and Destiny House

"*Builders and Blockers of Life* is an insightful look into the challenges that are presented to us all. The journey is fraught with many pitfalls, but here Randal merges his personal, educational, and ministerial experience with years of experience in the field of recovery to show how to both biblically and skillfully replace those pitfalls with promises. I find this book to be an essential read; its principles need to be applied as essentially!"

—*Michael Hankins*
Senior pastor, Church in the City
Rowlett, Texas

"Having worked in the addiction and mental health field for over a decade, I have had the pleasure of witnessing Randal's teachings change people's destinies, including mine. In *Builders and Blockers of Life*, Randal illustrates such a valuable and wonderfully honest way to accomplish goals, providing a spiritual guidebook for achieving your best you."

—*Rick McGuire*
Certified Alcohol and Drug Abuse Counselor

"After reading *Builders and Blockers of Life*, I realized how important it is to have all of its subject matter ready and available to use for everything I face. It gives you a detailed breakdown of how to overcome so many challenges. Randal's Scripture references fit so well and become new in light of what he says. I look forward to helping others by recommending this book to them, and I will definitely keep it close by as one of my personal guides."

—*Oz Fox*
Guitarist, Stryper

"Randal Smalls rocks! I have been very fortunate to have been blessed with Smalls' help and guidance during dark times of my wild life. I appreciate his amazing dedication to turning my life around. I found the real me again through our communication—he saved my life."

—*Wesley Scantlin*
Puddle of Mudd

"*Builders and Blockers of Life* has given me a great outlook on being able to support and share my dreams with the people I love, as well as how to help people who have lost their dreams. Outlining so many of the obstacles we encounter on a daily basis, Randal shows us how to handle those disappointments and enables us to make the turn from the negative into the positive. Randal Smalls—a man with a huge heart always allowing people to better themselves."

—*Pete "Luv" Farmer*
Music Executive / Artist Management

"I have personally seen the results produced by Randal Smalls' ministry through the many lives that have been healed and transformed. *Builders and Blockers of Life* provides an enlightening, powerful, and practical tool for achieving the life you've dreamed of. Randal's genuine, heartfelt approach will give you a new resolve to move beyond your past circumstances and into a better you!"

—*Sonny Arguinzoni Jr.*
Senior pastor and elder, Victory Outreach International

"This book is compelling. Filled with vivid illustrations and life experiences that provide the foundations to build a better life, it is an impressive read for gaining awareness, confidence, and clarity. As a health care professional and practicing dentist for twenty-four years, I will definitely recommend *Builders and Blockers of Life* to everyone, especially my patients."

—*Dr. James Fang, DDS*

"Randal Smalls' passionate commitment to helping recovering addicts in person and in writing is not just commendable, it is sometimes unfathomable. He is expertly trained and spiritually gifted in the area of breaking down barriers and getting to the real issues. I have no doubt that this is key to his success in turning around the lives of so many people who are riddled with the disease of addiction. Randal is absolutely one-of-a-kind."

—*Pamela Farmer*
Makeup Artist

"Randal Smalls has a gift to passionately reach into the human spirit, helping others find the true essence of one's self. This book teaches us to let go of the negative patterns that often keep us bound and leave us feeling defeated. I truly love the honesty and encouragement that *Builders and Blockers of Life* delivers, constantly reminding me of my worth and that God created us for greatness."

—*Kristi Minx*
Hairstylist

"As a teenager on the verge of going to college, I may seem like the last person to pick up *Builders and Blockers of Life* because, during my few years on earth, I haven't yet endured harsh struggles or faced some of the problems Smalls describes. Without giant chips on my shoulders, I approached the book as sort of a precautionary tale, and I soon realized that many parts did actually pertain to my life. I identified in myself some of the roots of behavior called "Builders" or "Blockers." The book was really an insightful guide for self-reflection, and I will definitely be taking all of the advice with me to college."

—*Lauren*
Student

"If books could be made mandatory, I would mandate *Builders and Blockers of Life*. Randal clearly understands how to help you on your journey to fulfilling your personal and professional dreams."

—*Scott Laing*
Co-Founder of Professionals on Purpose

"Randal is the real thing. He is full of wisdom and his words have always helped me—a lot! I was the child who was turned off by the dogma of Christianity, but Randal has another take on it that has resonated with me and I greatly appreciate that."

—*Paul Phillips*
Former guitarist for Puddle of Mudd, Operator, and Rev Theory
Certified Personal Trainer

"Randal Smalls' *Builders and Blockers of Life* is an insightful look at how we create the reasons for being unable to move forward in life and how we allow negative experiences to drive our future decisions. By reflecting about our life choices and decisions, the 'Builders' will overcome the 'Blockers' to help us become more aware of our responsibility for taking control of the choices we make every day."

—*Reggie Smith*
Speech-Language Pathologist

BUILDERS *and* BLOCKERS *of* LIFE

**OVERCOMING OBSTACLES
FOR A BETTER YOU**

RANDAL SMALLS

WHITAKER
HOUSE

BUILDERS AND BLOCKERS OF LIFE:
Overcoming Obstacles for a Better You

RandalSmalls.com
thebetterlifecoach@gmail.com

Photography by Kaliq Scott.

ISBN: 978-1-62911-771-3
eBook ISBN: 978-1-62911-772-0
Printed in the United States of America
© 2016 by Randal J. Smolchuck

Whitaker House
1030 Hunt Valley Circle
New Kensington, PA 15068
www.whitakerhouse.com

Library of Congress Cataloging-in-Publication Data (Pending)

1 2 3 4 5 6 7 8 9 10 11 ⨂ 23 22 21 20 19 18 17 16

For Adeana—
the one who embodies *my* Better Life.

ACKNOWLEDGMENTS

Mom and Dad (on both sides)—for giving me life, love, and inspiration.

Don Milam—the one who believed in the vision for this book, and for whom I will occasionally cheer for his Eagles!

Christine Whitaker, Tom Cox, and Whitaker House—for your willingness, passion, and perseverance to bring books like this to the world.

CONTENTS

INTRODUCTION:
HELP YOURSELF

"Are you a friend of Bill's?" a woman leaned over and asked me during a class. It was the first time I had been asked that question, so I had no idea which Bill she was talking about, since I knew several, and I wasn't sure how to answer. As I wondered about our mutual acquaintance, it hit me: she was talking about Bill W. from Alcoholics Anonymous (AA).

One of the original founders of this worldwide recovery movement was a man named Bill Wilson. Over time, AA participants have learned to identify others in the fellowship as "friends" of Bill, asking, "Are you a friend of Bill W.?" When I realized my classmate had asked me if I was in AA probably due to the nature of my comments during the class discussion, I told her that while I was not actively involved in AA, I had friends in the program and I had been working with people in recovery for many years.

"Recovery?" Yes. My studies and involvement in addiction treatment have prompted a lot of discussions about the growing need for recovery in almost every sector of society. My conversations with everyone from young students to gang members, housewives to prostitutes, and professional athletes and celebrities to clergymen have led me to realize that most people, whether actively involved in a 12-Step Recovery Program or not, whether they have admitted they have a problem or not, still need some form of recovery.

I say that because we all have issues and are recovering from something. Since that fateful day in the garden of Eden when Adam and Eve ate the forbidden fruit, we human beings have had setbacks and have been trying to recover what we've lost. Whether we've lost our innocence, a friendship, a job, money, marriage, or even the loss of self-respect, we long to recover our losses. Whether others have beaten us up or we beat ourselves up, we all want to "be better," or "[B]etter," in some area of life.

Just like you, I have stuff in my life that I don't like. Some of those things simply annoy me; others make me feel disappointed in myself, and sometimes downright ashamed. Fortunately, I'm better now than I've ever been, but only because I realized that no one on this planet is more concerned with my improvement than me. No one else can make me change for the better—I am responsible for helping myself. Whatever the bad habits or unwanted behavior patterns, whether a result of my own or someone else's bad choices, ultimately I am the one who has to take the initiative to do something about them. The old saying really is true: "If it is to be, it is up to me."

Norman Vincent Peale, twentieth-century father of positive thinking, provided one of my all-time favorite quotes when he said, "It's always too early to quit." That concise reminder inspires me to believe that even when a person's spirit is willing but his flesh is weak, if he decides that, no matter what, he is going to recover, with God's help, he *will*! With that determination, we can uncover the truth about ourselves—namely, that we have what it takes to make peace with the past so that we can make history! We can discover within ourselves a reservoir of strength and wisdom to wake us up from the nightmares so that we can get busy making our lives a dream come true. I've written this book to help you do just that. What you hold in your hands can be summed up in Home Depot's old slogan, "You can do it. We can help."

Every day, in one-on-one sessions and support groups all over the globe, people are admitting they need help and are gaining the strength they need to get better one day at a time. Along with such support, we must remember that, no matter where we are, we have the support of the One who *made* the globe—just by admitting our needs and asking for His help!

If things are going well for you right now and you simply want to get better, start by making a choice to continue improving. If you're in the middle of a crisis, don't waste this opportunity to learn from experience and put some new patterns in place. Whether you're in a substance-abuse relapse, a recession, or an abusive relationship, no matter what's going on, recovering the real you is possible when you *decide* it's possible. When you believe in yourself and ask God for help, anything can happen. A better life than you've dreamed of can actually become a reality.

"Life better than my dreams?" Yes, it really is possible. And when you think about dreams, consider that they are not only the ultimate, big-picture dreams that we all have daydreamed about. Sure, everyone can relate to those dreams of having it all. But there are also dreams that need our attention right now—those ones that we may not have even categorized as dreams. To simplify it, I've come to the conclusion that the best way to define a dream is "something that can be better tomorrow than it is today."

That brings us to the phrase "be better," or **[B]**etter. Periodically throughout this book, I will use this term, which has become the simple one-word summation of my life's purpose to help myself and to inspire others to do whatever it takes to make their dreams come true.

In the following pages is a collection of bright ideas in the form of stories, insights, and inspirations that shed light on some of the simplest ways we can help ourselves to [B]etter by making peace with the past so we can start enjoying the present and designing our future. Through the years, the [B]etter mentality has helped thousands improve the quality of their life, and has morphed into a motto I try to live by each day. And because I know it will help you, too, I'm passing the [B]etter Life Motto on to you now:

TODAY I WILL LIVE INSPIRED IN SPIRIT, MIND, AND BODY, SO THAT I WILL LEAVE A LEGACY OF BETTER LIFE TOMORROW

Go ahead, say it out loud now and start getting used to it. Now that you're getting the gist of where we are going, you can begin or continue on the journey to a better life. And keep in mind this introductory [B]etter one-liner that always applies:

IF YOU THINK YOU CAN OR CAN'T [B]ETTER, YOU'RE RIGHT.

# PART 1

THE MOMENT OF TRUTH:
KEEP TAKING CHANCES OR
MAKE BETTER CHOICES?

1

FOR BETTER

What will it look like when your dreams come true?

At least once a week for quite a few years, I have been posing that question to groups of every size in venues of every type. I usually follow the question with an invitation for all attendees to close their eyes and imagine what their lives would look and feel like if they woke up tomorrow morning and their dreams had come true. Through the years, I've seen more than a few blank looks, and heard some people express that they had no clue what a dream-come-true lifestyle would look like, because they had never thought about it. My response to those looks and comments has always been, "It is your life. Maybe it's time to *start* thinking about it."

Is that your life? Maybe you have never really given it too much thought. Or perhaps you used to think about it all the time when you were a kid. Hours were spent daydreaming about who you wanted to be, things you wanted to do, and places you wanted to go; but then, one day, you got in trouble for daydreaming, so you quit. Maybe incidents or accidents along the way have caused you to set aside your dreams because you don't think you qualify for those things any more.

If any of this is true for you, or if you're just not sure what you're aiming for during your time on this planet, let me ask you something: Do you want to just keep taking chances with what life dishes out to you? Are you satisfied with how your future will look if nothing changes? Or do you want to start making better choices that will allow you to get more of what you want out of life? Because you can, you know. You have the limitless expanse of your God-given imagination—a personal power tool to immediately start dismantling old barriers and begin framing new pictures of what you want to see in your future.

YOU HAVE THE LIMITLESS EXPANSE OF YOUR GOD-GIVEN IMAGINATION—A PERSONAL POWER TOOL TO IMMEDIATELY START DISMANTLING OLD BARRIERS AND BEGIN FRAMING NEW PICTURES OF WHAT YOU WANT TO SEE IN YOUR FUTURE.

Maybe you don't like how your body looks and feels right now. Quick! Close your eyes (it helps you to focus) and start imagining what you want your body to look like and what kinds of things you could do with a healthy body. Or are you completely sick of your job? Try it again. Close your eyes and imagine what you would do for a living if you could do anything. And so on. You can use this exercise to imagine any area of your life—spirituality, finances, relationships, anything.

This exercise is vital as you begin reading this book. You might want to start now by imagining what it would feel like to have finally made peace with your past. How would it feel to go through your days and nights without being haunted by that pain? As you stop obsessing over your past, you'll start noticing other areas that need attention, and it will energize you! So don't do it just once! Keep it up! If you keep envisioning your future as you work through this book, you'll start to move into new levels of contentment.

Over the years, I have had the wonderful privilege of listening to people report their progress of satisfying new career ventures, peace of mind, relationship sparks, or just outlandish and fun experiences, thanking me for challenging them to use their imagination to design a better life. One woman excitedly told me of landing her dream job which involved three things she was passionate about. She said, "I had never imagined anything like this was even possible until you challenged us to picture what life would look like if our dreams came true!"

"So, Randal," you ask, "are you saying that if I simply close my eyes and imagine stuff, it will just come to me?" No, of course not. That's just one step. Once you open your eyes, you'll have to plan, prepare, and act to make things happen. But at least you'll have a target. When you know what you're aiming for, it's a whole lot easier to hit. So why not let your imagination run free? If something superior is an option, why not take it?

Decisions, Decisions

Since the 1990s, in public and private sessions, I have been introducing people to simple strategies for life improvement in our curriculum called "The Better Life Course." In schools, churches, conferences, and recovery centers, I've explained that "life course" is a sociological term given to the stages of human life from birth all the way until death. Steering that life course for better or for worse, however, depends on the quality of our choices. And if I've noticed one common thread that runs through people everywhere from the Great White North to the land down under, it is that everyone needs help making choices.

Benjamin Franklin, one of the founding fathers of America, said, "Be always at war with your vices, at peace with your neighbors, and let every New Year find you a better man." And Jesus said, *"A thief is only there to steal and kill and destroy. I came so they can have real and eternal life, more and better life than they ever dreamed of"* (John 10:10 MSG). If, during the course of our life, we don't learn how to recover what has been stolen or destroyed by bad habits and addictions, we'll probably learn to just go through the motions to be religious—whether it takes the form of Christianity or a 12-Step Recovery Program—without actually recovering.

I imagine you picked up this book because you know there is more to life than what you've been experiencing. The problem is, the patterns of your past have held you back and taken you way off track. Though some bad breaks may have you feeling far from where you want to be, I want you to know that I believe in you and in your ability to make better choices. You may say, "You don't even know me." True. But I *do* know you're human, and within every one of us, regardless of circumstances, is a resilience to bounce back and become better than ever. That's the reason I've dedicated my life to coaching people to make better decisions so that they can chart their own better life course. I want to help you get to the point of loving yourself and valuing your life, family, and future so much that you can't help but make smarter, more informed, and more confident decisions. And who knows, maybe you'll find out what many others have discovered—that all you need to get back in the groove is just a few adjustments here and there.

I WANT TO HELP YOU GET TO THE POINT OF LOVING YOURSELF AND VALUING YOUR LIFE, FAMILY, AND FUTURE SO MUCH THAT YOU CAN'T HELP BUT MAKE SMARTER, MORE INFORMED, AND MORE CONFIDENT DECISIONS.

Just A Little Bit

I'll never forget the time I was about twelve years old and my dad let me drive his blue-and-white striped Chevy truck. We had just returned from the sawmill with a load of sawdust to be used as bedding in the horses' stalls and were standing in the bed of the pickup, shoveling it out into the storage area inside the barn. When we needed more room behind the truck to empty the rest of the load, my dad spoke the words I had always dreamed he'd say: "Go ahead and pull up the truck just a little bit."

He didn't have to tell me twice—I was so excited! I threw my shovel aside, hopped down off the tailgate, and ran to the cab. After opening the door, I slid into the driver's seat and, with a big smile on my face, turned the key! When the engine roared to life, I mimicked what I had seen my Dad do by putting my foot on the brake as I shifted into drive. Then, with probably an even bigger smile, I did what I had seen people do on TV shows like *The Dukes of Hazzard*—I stomped on the gas pedal!

The tires squawked, and the vehicle lunged forward with my dad holding on for dear life in the bed of the truck, yelling, "Whoa! Whoa!" Before I knew what was happening, we had slammed into the side of an empty stall, splintering a fence post and demolishing the rest of the wall. We came to a halt after I had slammed on the brakes, and I just sat there a bit shaken up. Then I heard my Dad utter in a much quieter and somewhat defeated-sounding tone, "I said 'just a little bit.'"

For years after that, the only thing I was allowed to drive was the lawn mower.

On the journey toward improving our choices for a better life, we will find ourselves in dilemmas and tight spots, and, more often than not, all that is needed is a little movement. Most of the time, we don't require some big, sweeping changes of absolutely everything all at once. We don't need to stomp on the gas pedal. Usually, just one or two things need adjustment.

For example, if you've been having trouble with a boyfriend, it's probably not necessary to declare that all men are dogs and vow never to date men again. Simply deleting a few phone numbers and improving your selection process would suffice. If you're overweight, cutting out all food from your diet is certainly not the answer—just *certain* foods. Or perhaps you went to church when you were young and didn't like it. Does that mean you should throw out the whole concept of organized religion, faith, and a relationship with God? Maybe a little forgiveness, mercy, and open-mindedness might be all that's needed to take you further than you think.

What is the quality of your life right now? Chances are, you don't need everything to change by tomorrow. So it's probably a good idea to start small; knowing a little bit will go a long way.

Bite-Size

When big chunks of life seem to be out of whack, we have to resist the urge to change everything all at once. I'm sure you've said before, "I'm so hungry I could eat anything." You go into a restaurant, and everything on the menu looks and sounds so amazingly delicious that you want it all! When that happens to me, I have a habit of ordering way too much food, then eating less than half of what is on my plate. Maybe that's what our parents were talking about when they told us we had eyes bigger than our stomachs.

Yet we do the same thing when we want our whole lives to change and try to do it all before the weekend! Starving for something different, we just jump in and try to change everything.

More often than not, though, trying to cook up an overnight overhaul is a recipe for disaster. The lack of instant results produces a flavorless dish of disappointment and, hopes dashed, may spoil any appetite for change altogether. With a bad taste left in our mouth, we may get so set in our ways that even a whiff of change makes us queasy, so we turn up our nose and run the other way.

Setting high, lofty goals and gaining immediate results may work occasionally for a very select few. But most of us, when it comes to improving anything, have to be careful not to bite off more than we can chew. We must pace ourselves. Each time we make a better choice, we take another bite out of large issues that have loomed over us for so long.

EACH TIME WE MAKE A BETTER CHOICE, WE TAKE ANOTHER BITE OUT OF LARGE ISSUES THAT HAVE LOOMED OVER US FOR SO LONG.

Altering our perspective about the pain of our past can be a daunting task. Trying to recover some dignity after so much has been stolen from us, or trying to regain self-respect after being stuck in self-destruct mode for so long can seem like too much work. Speaking of the undertaking of a massive rebuilding project with a small group of people, the ancient prophet Zechariah uttered a timeless bit of encouragement: *"Do not despise these small beginnings, for the LORD rejoices to see the work begin"* (Zechariah 4:10). Nineteenth-century poet Emily Dickinson must have been thinking the same thing when she said, "You can gain more control over your life by paying closer attention to the little things." After all, it's not the size or quality of our start that matters. History is filled with humble beginnings that turned into amazing journeys and destinations. To build our better life, we can always start right where we are and use what we have to begin the recovery process. And performing regular maintenance and making necessary adjustments to improve the quality of our lifestyles will eventually serve to satisfy our hunger for change.

Start Somewhere

The key to starting is to pick a place and start there. Like every runner who has ever raced knows, there has to be a starting line somewhere. As a runner myself, I had an unusual encounter one day while running around my neighborhood. I spotted a fellow runner approaching on the sidewalk who seemed to be struggling with every step. When I got close enough to wave, she smiled and weakly raised her hand to return the gesture. But when she waved, I could see a pack of cigarettes in her hand! I immediately realized why she had been laboring so hard. She probably had been out of breath and hadn't built up her wind yet.

Now, you may think I'm going to launch into a lecture about the dangers of smoking, but that's not what this book is about. Granted, smoking and running don't seem to be a very conducive combination, but at least she was running in between puffs. There was *movement*—even if it was just one small step at a time. For that, she gets an A for effort in my book.

Instead of simply starting somewhere, too many people think far too long about their decision to improve. They tell themselves they are waiting for the day they have conquered certain bad habits before they even attempt to address others. Sadly, in most cases, that day never comes, and the life they dreamed of fades further and further from view.

To help shake us loose from that kind of thinking, try this phrase I learned during my Sunday-school days: "God catches His fish before He cleans them." It means if we will come to God just as we are, hang-ups and all, He'll take us in with no questions asked. We don't have to fix everything on our own. Once we're in a relationship with Him, He will start transforming us more and more as we take one small step at a time. Before we even realize it, we will be thinking, feeling, acting, and even looking better! We can't let various imperfect areas in our lives stop other efforts to improve. If we'll start where we are and do what we're able, God will do the rest.

Get Your Hopes Up

Right now, you may be thinking that this all sounds good and motivational but you're still apprehensive, because you've tried to change before and it didn't stick. Perhaps you felt really let down, and now you just want to be realistic about what's possible. I get it. I want to be realistic, too. So before you just skip to another chapter or put the book down, let me tell you a story.

When I was a kid, my friends and I would go roller-skating a lot. The first Monday night of each month, our church would rent out the local roller rink and invite other churches in the area to join us for a regional "Skate Night." Whether racing around fast enough to get the roller referee to blow his whistle, playing video games and competing in pinball tournaments, or just eating a bunch of junk food at the snack shop, my buddies and I always had a blast. But the real highlight was when the DJ would start playing a slow song and announce the ultimate adolescent romantic rendezvous known as the "Couples Skate."

When we heard those words, Mark, John, Steve, Greg, and I knew that it was time to put up or shut up. You see, prior to that announcement, we would skate around the place, talking and teasing one another about which girl we wanted to ask out for that thrilling slow roll around the rink. From time to time, our choices were easy to make, because we had girlfriends whom we were required to ask or risk some real backlash. But, usually, we would eye some new girl we hadn't seen before or one of the older good-looking girls from youth group whom we all had been trying to muster up the courage to pop the big question: "Will you skate with me?"

There were plenty of taunts—"You're a chicken." "You'll never do it." "Don't get your hopes up"—lots of razzing went back and forth prior to the proposals. But it all was *so* worth it when one of us would finally take the risk, roll up to the girl, put it all on the line, and she'd say "yes." After all these years, I'm still pretty proud to report that, on several occasions, I had that amazing satisfaction of taking the object of my desire by the hand, escorting her onto the wooden floor, and making small talk with her as we slowly rolled around and around. In the dark, under the dancing lights of the disco ball, gliding past my friends still on the sidelines, it was hard to hide my huge glowing smile.

THE STRONGER OUR HOPE, THE BRAVER WE ARE; AND THE BRAVER WE ARE, THE MORE WE ATTEMPT AND ACCOMPLISH, RESULTING IN A WEALTH OF EXPERIENCE.

I wasn't aware of it then, but now I know what made that huge smile and feeling of accomplishment possible—hope. If I hadn't had any hope that the girl would say yes, I never would have been able to scrounge up the audacity to approach her. Research shows that no matter the situation, hope always empowers. The stronger our hope, the braver we are; and the braver we are, the more we attempt and accomplish, resulting in a wealth of experience. At one time or another, though, we all have been in the line of fire of the soul-crushing words, "Don't get your hopes up." Perhaps they were directed at you as a kid nearing Christmastime when your parents heard about that high-priced hot-toy-of-the-year you wanted from Santa. They might have been spoken to you as a teenager when your friends found out that you liked that certain guy or girl in your class. Maybe somebody dashed your hopes when you declared that you would break a bad habit. Crushing words or sentiments can come from any source at any time, and, unfortunately, the most frequent voice we hear stamping out our hopes is our own. It blares obnoxiously at us all hours of the day and night, our own internal loudspeaker booming, *Who do you think you are? That'll never happen! You can't do it! Don't even try! Be realistic!*

How many times have you started out with bold intentions to renovate something in your life when, all of a sudden, your internal PA system kicks in with hope-killing propaganda about how ill-equipped you are to even consider that anything different is possible? That mental boom box starts reverberating a beat that numbs your resolve, accompanied by a repetitive loop of horribly depressing lyrics commemorating past miserable failures: "Rejected!" "Cheater!" "Liar!" "Fired!" "Addict!" "Bankrupt!" "Thief!" "Stupid!" And on and on it goes.

How do we get over the hump? What will it take for us to pull the plug on that nonstop nonsense? For my money, you can't go wrong with the electric power of hope. When you truly tap in to that constant current of *belief* that things will not always be this way, it will produce heat. Then that life-altering belief will start melting doubt and lifting confidence to the surface. I can find no better confidence than in the words of St. Paul: *"Therefore, we who have fled to him for refuge can have great confidence as we hold to the hope that lies before us. This hope is a strong and trustworthy anchor for our souls"* (Hebrews 6:18–19).

Even if you're still unsure, great confidence *is* available. It's an invaluable element of a well-lived life built by one choice at a time while holding onto the anchor of a strong hope. So where will you tune in and turn up? Will you tune in to your harshest critic, or will you tune in to what sounds like music to your ears? If you decide to do what's best for you, your family, and your future, you'll start getting your hopes up!

2

RESULTS MAY VARY

The question "Do you want to get well?" is music to my ears, and is quoted in one of my favorite Bible stories. It's the question Jesus asked a man who had been crippled for thirty-eight years. In spite of his lame legs, the man had somehow made his way to the pool of Bethesda, in Jerusalem, which supposedly had healing waters. Legend had it that an angel would occasionally disturb the water, and the first person into the pool afterward was healed of his sickness. Apparently, stories of healing traveled, because people came from far and wide to gather around that pool to watch and wait for the water to move.

I give the lame man credit for making it to the pool. No doubt the healing water had piqued his interest. Most likely, he was dissatisfied with his low quality of life, and the possibility of a better life was probably a huge breath of fresh air. It sparked something in him to imagine that he didn't have to stay crippled after all; that things could actually be different for him and for his family. He must have believed the legend, or at least was hopeful enough to make a move. Perhaps his own small movements, slowly shuffling along the dusty ground, got him to the water's edge, or maybe he found others to help move him; regardless, his determination eventually got him to the healing pool.

Imagine finally being among the crowd at Bethesda. At first, just the change of scenery and being around all the people had to be exciting. Then, he was probably thrilled to discover that people in the city regularly dropped money on the mats of the sick folks around the pool. Hearing eyewitness stories about the miracle properties of the water probably had an energizing effect—for a while.

After some time, the zeal probably started to wear off. I imagine it became a bit disheartening to see so many people jockeying for position near the pool when healing only occasionally happened, all the while wondering if it ever really even happened at all. Was it all just an urban legend?

But he kept his eyes glued on the water, and as a year went by, I imagine he settled into a new line of thinking: *I sure hope this works! But how will I ever get through all these people to get to the water?* Three years, *It's not fair that I get pushed out of the way.* Then six years flew by. At this point, he probably was not as focused on the water as he had been in the past: *People are so selfish. Nobody will even help me.* Nine years, fifteen, *Yes, I can still see the pool from over here.* Eighteen years, twenty-six years, *I don't know why these people still get so excited over a little ripple of water.* Then twenty-seven years, thirty-two, thirty-six, thirty-eight years laying on his mat near the pool of healing water.

Be Reasonable

One reason I am so fond of this story is that I see in it some parallels to our own lives. We get excited by the possibility of upgrading, and with the best of intentions, quickly bust a move or two to get ourselves into position for it to happen. But if it doesn't go as quickly as we'd like, or it requires more work than we'd thought, we settle in and start to get comfortable. Even though the situation is actually quite *uncomfortable* and we are still dissatisfied with our condition, it is still familiar, so we don't do much about it—except complain. We know how to navigate the surroundings and what stories to tell to keep ourselves and others believing that this is the best we can do because of all that has or hasn't happened in the past. I've seen it many times through the years as "The Better Life Coach." People start attending group or personal sessions but then drop out after the realization that it may not go exactly as they had planned or that it will require some actual effort on their part.

But back to the story. One day, the man who had come to the pool with high hopes so many years earlier was suddenly startled by an inquiry from a stranger—a guy named Jesus. He probably thought, *Wait, is He talking to me? Who is this Man standing in front of me, anyway? He's obviously not from this town. I think He asked if I want to get well. What kind of question is that? I'm here at the pool, aren't I?* Then he responds to Jesus' question, saying, "I can't, sir...for I have no one to put me into the pool when the water bubbles up. Someone else always gets there ahead of me" (John 5:7).

All too frequently, that's what we do—make excuses. Now before you start to run down the list of why your excuses are valid, let me tell you, I agree. I don't doubt they are legitimate. I believe you're telling the truth, because I have listened to far too many unthinkable, horrendous stories of what people have had to endure. I would never act as if you don't have good reasons for feeling or acting the way you do. I am truly very sorry you've had to go through that pain, and I sincerely hope and pray this book will help you deal with it effectively.

But here's my question: How long will those excuses remain valid? Could it be that expiration notices have been issued on those old stories of who did or didn't do something to you or for you? Maybe those stories of abandonment and betrayal didn't quite seem to cut it the last few times you told them. They didn't ring true, or it felt like they had lost their power. Maybe the clue was that look on someone's face after you had told him the same old story for the umpteenth time, as if to say, "Really? You're talking about *this* again?"

The lame man may have gotten that look from the out-of-towner that day, because the story says, *"When Jesus saw him and knew he had been ill for a long time, he asked him, 'Would you like to get well?'"* (John 5:6, emphasis added). Looking at the man's living situation, seeing that he had settled into an uncomfortable but familiar routine, Jesus was essentially asking the man, "Is getting well even something you're still interested in?" I've often thought about how this question applies to our lives, too, especially in regard to my mission of helping people improve their decision-making. I could just rephrase it this way: "Do *you* want a better life?"

At that moment, the lame man was presented with an opportunity to stop taking chances and start making better choices. As he issued his normal excuses, he heard his words fall flat. They didn't have the same effect on this Man that they usually had on others. This Man's face was compassionate, yet it looked as if He was expecting action, not words. The Bethesda-pool veteran found himself in a moment that just felt *different*.

Click

I've had moments like that, and I bet you have, too. I remember one of the times, when the thought *I can't keep doing this* kept running through my head as I sped north on the freeway toward Tennessee with my buddy and our girlfriends. We were in our late teens and were driving back to Michigan after spending spring break in Florida. It had been a fun time at the beach, partying and doing what teenagers do on spring break, but as we crossed the Florida-Georgia state line, an unsettling feeling started brewing somewhere down inside of me.

I remember my mind racing, and I was strangely quiet for quite a long time as we wound our way through the mountains, dissatisfaction working its way through me. It's really difficult to put it into words, but the air just felt heavier. I was in a stage of adolescence when I made every possible excuse to avoid spending time with my family so I could be with my friends, with whom I was often up to no good. None of us had ever gotten into any real serious trouble, but that growing dissatisfaction inside of me had me feeling like all that was about to change, unless *I* changed.

It was like I started having a premonition that if I didn't do an about-face on my knuckleheaded ways, what I had considered edgy fun would soon become a problem for me. I didn't know all the details about what would happen to me if I didn't make changes, and I didn't have a road map on *how* to change; I just knew that if I didn't do something, I was headed for trouble.

On that fateful car ride up I-75, though I didn't realize it at the time, I had a moment of truth, much like the lame man at the pool of Bethesda. Those moments have been described by some as instances of total clarity, or an epiphany or revelation, like seeing or understanding something so clearly for the first time. When we gain awareness or grasp some new knowledge that we know in our hearts to be true, though it may be hard to admit or accept, we are facing a moment of truth. Some moments pass in a flash. Some are longer than others, lasting hours, a few days, or as mine did, maybe even longer. How long they last, though, is not as important as what we do during those times.

WHEN WE GAIN AWARENESS OR GRASP SOME NEW KNOWLEDGE THAT WE KNOW IN OUR HEARTS TO BE TRUE, THOUGH IT MAY BE HARD TO ADMIT OR ACCEPT, WE ARE FACING A MOMENT OF TRUTH.

Many of us have heard that when we *"know the truth, the truth will set* [us] *free"* (John 8:32), but the actual freedom comes only when we do something with that truth. When a lightbulb of truth (or what I call a "lifebulb") clicks on in our heads, and we accept it and believe it in our hearts, it will start to affect what we do with our hands. If we do nothing with lifebulbs of truth—those things that suddenly make sense or just keep popping up in our consciousness—we may be tightening the lock on our own prison.

I imagine that after the lame man had finished delivering his excuses and sensed something different about the out-of-towner, the air charged and the moment electric, he had an exasperated look on his face. Maybe, as he realized that this was *his* chance, the standard look in his eyes, which had, for so long, elicited pity and donations from strangers, suddenly turned into a look of desperation, revealing his internal plea: *I can't keep doing this. Can you help me?* We know that something must have happened, because without acknowledging the man's same old excuses, Jesus simply said, *"Stand up, pick up your mat, and walk!"* (John 5:8).

Missed Opportunities

It's scary to think of what could happen if we pass up moments of truth. I watched that very thing happen one day at Starbucks. In the middle of

enjoying my coffee with a friend on the patio, I felt like someone was star-
ing at us. Sure enough, when I turned my head, I saw a man standing just
behind me, who asked, "Could I borrow fifty cents?" When I asked him
what he needed it for, he launched into a story about how he had some
gospel material he wanted to read, but he needed new glasses to see it.
I realized that he had been eavesdropping on our conversation; my missionary friend had been talking about an overseas gospel campaign that
included the distribution of printed materials. So I thought about giving
this stranger something just for being creative with his pitch for money.

But as he continued to talk, explaining about how his worsening eye-
sight had forced him to quit the family business of cutting hair, I realized he was a friend of a friend! I remembered my friend's stories about
all the attempts he had made through the years to help this man in his
fight against alcoholism. So, naturally, this stranger looked shocked when
I asked him, "Is alcohol still a problem for you, Philip?"

His countenance fell and he slowly nodded, so I offered, "Do you want
help today?" I told him I could get him right into a men's recovery center,
free of charge.

"Which one?" he asked.

When I told him the name of the Christ-centered facility, he balked.
"Oh, no. I'm not going there. All that God stuff doesn't work."

I replied, "Didn't you just tell us that you wanted to read some gospel
material?"

Realizing that he had contradicted his pitch for money, he started to
explain his bizarre theory that God couldn't exist and that there is no higher power that could help him. He just kept babbling on and on, getting
more agitated by the minute, until I finally stopped him.

"Philip, you're not going to get anywhere arguing with a minister and a
missionary that God doesn't exist. I believe God set up this moment for us
to meet and offer you a shot at a better life today, but it's obvious you don't
want to change. Now, I haven't seen my friend in a while, and we have only
a short time left to talk, so unless you want to accept the offer, we're going
to get back to our conversation."

He just huffed, "No way!" and hurried around the corner, out of sight.

It was sad to see, but Philip didn't recognize he'd had a moment of truth that could have set him free, and he walked away from it. Have you ever done that? I think it's happened to all of us at least once. Not until afterward do we realize, in the clarity of hindsight, that we missed a golden opportunity because we weren't paying attention or just didn't feel any urgency at the time.

A glaring lack of urgency was what I saw one morning at the gym. I heard the woman at the front desk frantically say into the phone, "Yes, we need an ambulance right away!" Evidently, someone in one of the locker rooms in the back of the building needed urgent medical attention. Sure enough, a few minutes later, from my spot on the elliptical machine, I saw an ambulance pull up to the front door. But then an unusual scene unfolded.

As I watched the first paramedics enter the doors with a gurney and all their equipment and start toward the locker rooms, I thought it looked odd for some reason. Then I realized it *was* odd, because they were walking unusually slowly! They just strolled along, looking around the workout floor, glancing into the aerobics room, peeking into the spin class, as if they were on a new-members tour. Then came another set of medical personnel walking into the gym, and they, too, just sauntered through, looking disinterested, moving as if their feet were stuck in saltwater taffy! All the while, from what I understood, someone in the back of that building was still in need of urgent care.

What I witnessed that day could be applied to our own lives. It may not concern a physical issue like that person in the locker room or the lame man at the pool, or even an addiction like Philip's, but we know we have an area or two that are in desperate need of attention. Yet we just keep moseying along, seemingly oblivious, acting as if we have all the time we need and don't have a care in the world. As I said, I think we've all done it. You know how it goes. We wait for the perfect time, worry about what people will think, and drag our feet because we're unsure what we'll be getting ourselves in to.

The surprising thing is that when we finally do dive into the issue at hand, it is often less painful than we imagined. I think that's what happened with the paramedics at the gym. They had probably gotten word that whatever trouble the person was having was not so bad after all. That's why they were so casual in their approach. But you and I are still not off the hook. If we'll turn our attention to where it's needed, addressing the issue at hand, we may even discover that it is not so scary after all; it may actually feel good. Self-care is not a sin, but avoiding it might be.

Easy as ABC

Making improvements in our lives often doesn't seem urgent because we psych ourselves out and make it harder than it has to be. In this way, we are kind of like the folks from previous generations who claim that, back in their day, they didn't have it so easy. You know the sort: "In my day, we had to walk five miles to and from school. Every single day! In the snow! And it was uphill both ways!"

Uphill both ways—isn't that physically impossible? Maybe not. I wonder about it, because if you're like me, at times it can feel like life is all uphill, and because it seems so hard, we don't have an urgency to do anything. It's as if we're continuously climbing and climbing and climbing and never get a break. Like when we try to climb a ladder to a certain career position, or initiate or improve a relationship, or increase our income while stretching our current cash flow. Then when we approach what we think is the top, something goes awry, and we realize it's not a pinnacle at all—there's no downhill in sight! So we keep climbing.

I've never gone rock climbing, so I don't know very much about it, but I do know that it is absolutely essential to have rope. If you're going to climb very high, you must have something to hold on to for security, something with which to pull yourself or fellow climbers up. If you think about it, in our daily ascent toward a better life, we need a rope called *faith*. If we can't glimpse the top, it's okay. According to the apostle Paul, *"Faith is the confidence that what we hope for will actually happen; it gives us assurance about things we cannot see"* (Hebrews 11:1).

Faith starts when we get our hopes up about something, which initiates the need to climb. However, that wonderful ability to believe what we can't see is like a muscle; it is stretched and strengthened only when pressure is applied. And when the cliff seems too steep, the weight seems too great, and there's no clear view of how far to the next plateau, the only thing that will hold us in place is the confidence that our hopes will be fulfilled. Sometimes that assurance comes from within. Sometimes it comes from fellow climbers—some of whom are on the journey with you, and some of whom have gone before you. But the ultimate assurance comes from the One who gave us the desire to climb in the first place.

FAITH STARTS WHEN WE GET OUR HOPES UP ABOUT SOMETHING, WHICH INITIATES THE NEED TO CLIMB.

Most of us have desired to move up higher for as long as we can remember—right? It's elementary. But if we're actually going to make that happen, it's absolutely essential that we capitalize on those *clicks*, or moments of truth. We'll find new freedom if we accept and act on these truths. So I've come up with something easy to help us remember what to do in those moments.

There's nothing much simpler than the ABCs. Remember when you first learned to recite them? Most children's alphabet recitals never end with the letter Z; they are always followed by, "Now I know my ABCs; next time won't you sing with me?" At the time, kids have no idea that an entire lifetime of possibilities have been opened up to them just by getting familiar with those twenty-six little letters!

Now, after years of you using those letters to help you get around on this planet, I want to introduce you to another set of ABCs that very well may open up another world of possibilities to you. I call them **"The ABCs of a Better Life."** Our new set of ABCs reads like this:

+ A is for *Admit.*

+ B is for *Believe.*

+ C is for *Choose.*

Individually, each admission, belief, and choice can be an effective agent of change. But together, they become a very powerful formula for growth.

You see, if you and I are going to entertain the notion of helping ourselves, we have to *admit* that we have issues that need our attention and that we want more out of life. Admission is the first step for absolutely anything. I mean, the first step of getting a sandwich is admitting you're hungry! Then, in order for any changes to occur, we must *believe* we can change. Belief in ourselves is a great start, but when we involve our spirits by believing and trusting God, we become anchored by a growing expectation that all things are possible, and a growing assurance that we can handle anything. And belief takes on a new level of effectiveness when we *choose* to do whatever it takes to effect the change we want to see. These three actions will prove to be extremely valuable not only as we make peace with the past but as we take each step along the journey to making our dreams come true. We can use these vital tools at any time to make sure we stay on course.

IF YOU AND I ARE GOING TO ENTERTAIN THE NOTION OF HELPING OURSELVES, WE HAVE TO *ADMIT* THAT WE HAVE ISSUES THAT NEED OUR ATTENTION AND THAT WE WANT MORE OUT OF LIFE. ADMISSION IS THE FIRST STEP FOR ABSOLUTELY ANYTHING.

It's likely that some things in the first two chapters have *clicked* for you (which will continue to occur as you keep reading). Perhaps you've realized that *now* is the time for change, and perhaps you are more than ready to make peace with your past. That means that *now* is also the perfect time to start practicing the ABCs of a Better Life. Start by answering the following questions:

+ What do I need to admit? What are some things I absolutely must change?

+ What do I believe is possible? What do I want out of life?

+ What do I choose to do about it?

There's no doubt good things will come as we practice these ABCs.

BUILDERS AND BLOCKERS:
DOUBT VERSUS BELIEF

Whenever we are presented with the opportunity to advance, what I call a "better-life blocker" usually shows up to try to keep us from making any progress. In moments of truth, we are often faced with the better-life blocker of *doubt*.

Doubt

The definition of doubt is "to be uncertain about; consider questionable or unlikely; hesitate to believe...a feeling of uncertainty about the truth."[1]

To discover whether doubt may be blocking you, consider this brief description and the types of behavior it may spark in us. Do you see yourself in any of the following?

How Doubt Looks and Acts

A person with doubt may be ambiguous, apprehensive, confused, cynical, distrustful, faithless, hesitant, indecisive, reluctant, skeptical,

---

1. "doubt," *Dictionary.com*, http://www.dictionary.com/browse/doubt?s=t.

suspicious, wavering, or lacking confidence. This person may distrust leaders, family members (including spouse), coworkers, neighbors, and friends. They are commonly suspicious of people; often think or say, "I won't believe it until I see it"; and are hesitant to make or keep commitments. This person has limited plans, visions, or goals for the future. They are unconvinced of God's love, and susceptible to feelings of worthlessness.

Make It Personal

Resist the urge to think about someone else this may apply to. Be honest—this is about you. Take a moment to list any ways you see doubt evident in your present behavior.

Belief

In order to recover what we've lost, we need what I call "better-life builders." During moments of truth, we absolutely must have *belief*, "an opinion or conviction…confidence in the truth or existence of something not immediately susceptible to rigorous proof…faith; trust."[2] Which of the following characteristics of belief are you most interested in developing?

How Belief Looks and Acts

A person with belief can be accepting, assured, certain, expectant, hopeful, persuaded, and reliant on someone or something. This person trusts in leadership, is confident in their support system, gives others the benefit of the doubt, and trusts and believes others.

They are not apprehensive to make or keep commitments, and their body language suggests confidence. They make plans, set goals, and have a vision for the future. They are confident, assured, and convinced of their self-worth and of God's love.

Belief Building Material

Repetition builds skill. So take time daily to build your better life by thinking, praying, and/or saying the following truths about belief:

2. "belief," *Dictionary.com*, http://www.dictionary.com/browse/belief.

Jesus looked at them and said, "With man this is impossible, but not with God; all things are possible with God." (Mark 10:27 NIV)

Truly I tell you, if anyone says to this mountain, "Go, throw yourself into the sea," and does not doubt in their heart but believes that what they say will happen, it will be done for them. (Mark 11:23 NIV)

"We are what we believe we are."
—C. S. Lewis

"When you believe in a thing, believe in it all the way."
—Walt Disney

Make It Personal

Where do you need to exercise belief? Before moving on, take some time to practice the "3-R's": reflect, release, and renew. Ask yourself the following questions and then apply them to your life.

Reflect

1. What was the most interesting part of what I just read?
2. What would it look like for my dreams come true?
3. What small adjustments would make a big difference for me?
4. What do I hope will happen in my life?
5. What hope-crushing words do I tell myself?
6. What moments of truth have I had?

Release

If there is anything you need to let go of, repeat the following: "After reflecting, I see that I need to let go of _____, and I choose to release it now." Then pray this Scripture over your life:

> *Create in me a clean heart, O God; and renew a right spirit within*
> *me.*   (Psalm 51:10 KJV)

Renew

After releasing what's been weighing on you, what are some positive things you can commit to in the future?

> *You will know the truth, and the truth will set you free.*   (John 8:32)

PART 2

BACKGROUND CHECK: CAN UNDERSTANDING MY PAST HELP MY FUTURE?

3

◤ LESSONS LEARNED

In the early 1990s, the late comedian Chris Farley acted in a recurring skit on *Saturday Night Live* called *The Chris Farley Show*, in which he would interview well-known celebrities in an awkward, fumbling manner. He played a nervous, fidgety, completely insecure type, opposite the calm, confident, famous interviewee. What made it so funny was that several times in each episode, Chris would ask a question or comment on some common knowledge about the guest, to which the guest would give a deadpan, somewhat sarcastic reply. Upon realizing that he had just asked a question to which the entire world already knew the answer, Chris would then look away from the guest, smack himself on the forehead, pull his hair, and grumble, "What an idiot! I am so stupid! What a stupid, stupid question!" The celebrity would then try to reassure Chris that he was doing okay and encourage him to keep the interview going. Eventually, Chris would compose himself and try again. It was hilarious to watch.

It's anything but funny, though, when episodes in our past make us feel super self-conscious. Most of us are way too hard on ourselves about what we've been through. Oh, we may not be the Chris-Farley-type, smacking ourselves on the head or grumbling about how stupid we are (although some do, and, sadly, some do even worse); but we punish ourselves silently for past incidents and accidents, whether self-inflicted or dished out to us by others. If an amplifier was designed to broadcast our thoughts, we'd hear how so many negative messages repeating in our heads are badgering put-downs about how dumb, ugly, unwanted, or unholy we are—all related to a list of not-so-shiny moments from our past.

Highs and Lows

Encountering and overcoming tremendous adversity after going blind and deaf at a very young age, Helen Keller became an inspiration to millions of people around the world throughout the twentieth and twenty-first century—well beyond her passing in 1968. Her story and insight, gained from pushing through her own daunting challenges, have always personally challenged me. She often quoted something that Ralph Waldo Emerson once said: "Life is a succession of lessons which must be lived to be understood." This quote has stuck with me, and has not only been a catalyst for altering the way I view the good and bad events of my own life but also for discussion on new ways to view the pain of the past. Past pain doesn't have to remain painful; we can alter our perspectives by viewing it as a lesson.

PAST PAIN DOESN'T HAVE TO REMAIN PAINFUL; WE CAN ALTER OUR PERSPECTIVES BY VIEWING IT AS A LESSON.

See, our current state of affairs is a result of where we've been, what we've done, and whom we've been with up to this point. Life as we know it is the total sum of our experiences. Our lessons have made us who we are today. "All our born days," as my mom used to say, we have experienced what Frank Sinatra sang about in "That's Life." He crooned, "You're riding high in April, shot down in May" and later, "back on top, *back on top* in June."[3]

---

3. Vernon Duke, E. Y. Harburg, "That's Life," (Warner/Chappell Music, Inc., Universal Music Publishing Group, 1966).

The highs and lows we experience are par for the course on this planet. The problem we repeatedly run into is paying too much attention to, and spending too much energy on, the downturns. Hurt, shock, anger, loneliness, sadness, depression, and outrage are common emotions when we experience pain. However, dwelling on the negative occurrences and emotions for extended periods of time will progressively darken our self-image, as well as our thought and speech patterns.

If we don't learn lessons from our experiences, we run the risk of developing a victim mentality and vocabulary. When we view ourselves, experiences, and surroundings in a bad light, we have a tendency to overreact and become irrational. And as we keep expecting poor treatment and claiming discrimination, our words grow increasingly negative.

Laundry List

Once, in need of some clean clothes, I hurriedly sorted out what I needed from the clothes hamper, added the detergent, and fabric softener into the washing machine, and started it. After what seemed like an eternity, the machine finally finished its cycle, and I rushed to transfer the clothes to the dryer. There was only one problem: the washer was empty! I panicked for a second and thought, *Who stole my clothes right out of this machine?* But there was a hole in that theory—I was home, alone.

Standing outside the laundry room, completely baffled about the missing clothes, I tilted my head and put on my best crime-solving hat. Then, out of the corner of my eye, something caught my attention—the pile of laundry! There it was, still dirty, sitting on top of the bed, right where I had left it when I hurried down the hallway to start the machine. As you can imagine, I felt completely stupid for a minute, but then I shook my head and laughed, thankful that nobody had been there to witness my absent-minded move.

We all do dumb things from time to time. No matter how well put together we are, there will always be surprises. Occasionally, there will be pleasant surprises, but often there will be bad surprises. We all have been surprised by things we've done that we wish we hadn't. Other times, people blindside us, bringing on horribly unpleasant circumstances. Once, when I was going through a nightmarish situation that had hit me out of left field, my dad made a statement that stuck with me ever since: "Son, I guess it's all in how you view it."

Now, at that time, I felt sad, betrayed, and a whole laundry list of other negative emotions, and I wondered if there even *was* any other way to view what had happened. But I slowly started to see what my father had meant. I stopped feeling so sorry for myself long enough to notice other people who were experiencing even worse situations than me. Though I was still hurting, my "woe is me," "it's not fair" mentality began to wear thin. I started thanking God that I wasn't alone, that I had Him and others like my dad to help me through it. As I fought through the haze of self-pity, and shifted my focus away from whining and toward learning, pearls of wisdom started to emerge.

Moving Out

If you and I are going to move in to a better life, one of the first things we have to do is begin breaking some bad habits. We must move out of the complaining stage, removing "It's not fair" from our mentality and vocabulary. We complain and blame others for our raw deal, but we simply must erase that scarlet letter V for victim and L for loser from our forehead. Playing the victim is one of those bad habits some of us have developed in an attempt to find value and love, but if we stay in that mind-set too long, we go from being a victim to a volunteer. If we don't alter our outlook so we can learn something from our trials, then just like that man at the pool of Bethesda, we will end up voluntarily staying in the same uncomfortable position!

PLAYING THE VICTIM IS ONE OF THOSE BAD HABITS SOME OF US HAVE DEVELOPED IN AN ATTEMPT TO FIND VALUE AND LOVE, BUT IF WE STAY IN THAT MIND-SET TOO LONG, WE GO FROM BEING A VICTIM TO A VOLUNTEER.

The apostle Paul complained to God about his uncomfortable position, or his "thorn in the flesh" (see 2 Corinthians 12:7), as he called it. He earnestly asked God three different times to take the pain away from him. Do you know what God's response was? He said, *"My grace is sufficient for you, for my power is made perfect in weakness"* (2 Corinthians 12:9 NIV). Apparently, Paul got the message, because he responded, *"That is why, for Christ's sake, I delight in weaknesses, in insults, in hardships, in persecutions, in difficulties. For when I am weak, then I am strong"* (2 Corinthians 12:10 NIV).

That response has always encouraged me. Perhaps you're a lot like me, knowing that you have a very long way to go before you can truly delight in your difficulties. But we can certainly get a big pick-me-up by remembering that when we feel weak, we are perfect candidates for God's grace and strength!

Paul gained a vast amount of confidence and learned lessons from the life dealt out to him, including being ostracized and facing unjust persecution. His bumpy background allowed him to write one of the most motivational passages of all time while wrongfully imprisoned: *"I have learned the secret of being content in any and every situation…. I can do all this through him who gives me strength"* (Philippians 4:12–13 NIV).

I once listened to a twenty-something girl admit that she had done a lot of unsafe and stupid things during her teenage years. She wasn't proud of what she'd done, but she indicated that those things no longer held any attraction for her; she had a "been there, done that" perspective, and felt that she had really gotten it out of her system. Because of how far she'd come, she felt good talking about her experiences. It allowed her to shift her focus from her past to the present, which involved finishing college and becoming a responsible adult.

We've done things, or others have done things to us, that we aren't proud of; maybe they weren't our smartest moves, or we were victimized in some way, but at least now we know some of what we absolutely do not want in our future. Thank God we've had some of these experiences, because now we have a unique ability to relate to others who are struggling.

What would have happened if the apostle Paul hadn't learned his lessons? I'm pretty sure he would not have had such a huge impact on human history. He has instructed, challenged, and motivated generations of people, all by just sharing his experiences. I wonder who you could influence by shifting out of victim mode and into victor mode. There are people in our life right now who are waiting for us to learn our lessons so we can help them learn theirs, too. Nothing we go through, whether good times or bad, will be wasted if we learn to look at it as a lesson.

NOTHING WE GO THROUGH, WHETHER GOOD
TIMES OR BAD, WILL BE WASTED IF
WE LEARN TO LOOK AT IT AS A LESSON.

Something for the Pain

Talk about good times and bad—one day I performed a wedding ceremony, and the next day I spoke at a funeral, providing a lesson in dizzying emotional extremes. It felt like that famous line in *A Tale of Two Cities* by Charles Dickens: "It was the best of times, it was the worst of times." Long before Dickens wrote that, King Solomon wrote, *"There is a time for everything, and a season for every activity under the heavens:…a time to mourn and a time to dance"* (Ecclesiastes 3:1, 4 niv).

We all have seen people at wedding receptions laughing, dancing, and partying. People never seem to require any instruction on how to have a good time at such occasions. Celebrating life milestones like marriage, job promotions, bonuses, or a new baby is instinctive; we are happy when the circumstances are happy and spirits are high.

It is during the down times that we need extra support—sometimes just to make it through the night. When our past haunts us, or when we encounter morbid realities like the untimely death of a loved one, downsizing, a messy divorce, or a financial disaster, we desperately need comfort and coaching on how to cope. When we are at our lowest, we simply must have some reassurance that some good will eventually come out of what is currently so bad.

Some comfort may be drawn from the simple but true phrase "This too shall pass," but while waiting for that to happen, we need not run from the pain. It is okay, and actually part of the healing process, to feel hurt and allow pain to force out hard feelings.

One time in Indonesia, I stood at a safe distance watching my friend howl in pain as a reflexology specialist kneaded the bottom of his foot. In a kind gesture, our hosts had brought over their favorite massage therapist to demonstrate how to release pressure and relieve pain. One thing they had failed to mention, though, was how painful the process could be. "Please tell him it hurts," my buddy begged our host to tell the masseuse, who didn't speak a word of English.

Our host replied matter-of-factly, "It will hurt."

"But I don't want it to hurt," pleaded my friend.

Our Indonesian host replied a little more emphatically this time, "It will hurt," as if to say, "That's part of the deal." Pain is part of the process in this healing remedy.

When you think about it, if given the choice, nobody in his right mind wants to go through pain. It doesn't matter when or where it comes from; whether it's physical or emotional pain; whether related to a job, relationships, finances, or any other kind of nagging discomfort—everyone would choose the path of no pain if it were possible. But, sadly, it is unavoidable. And, as we read in James chapter 1, avoidance is not in our best interest after all:

Consider it a sheer gift, friends, when tests and challenges come at you from all sides. You know that under pressure, your faith-life is forced into the open and shows its true colors. So don't try to get out of anything prematurely. Let it do its work so you become mature and well-developed, not deficient in any way. (James 1:2–4 MSG)

So as it turns out, for those of us actively seeking to make peace with our past, dark times can actually be gold mines. A shining example of this has been Joyce Meyer, who has bravely shared her personal struggles and used them as teaching points, to which multitudes relate through her daily media presence. She has shown that when situations turn sharp and keep stabbing us in the heart, we are led through a sifting process that reveals extremely valuable nuggets of character. Any stories that emerge from grappling with almost unbearable pain not only enrich our own mindfulness and gratitude but boost our confidence. Like the apostle Paul, we believe that if we can make it through *that*, we can make it through anything. Stories with rich plot lines are rarely kept under wraps, and each time they are told and retold, they increase in value both to the one who tells it and to all those who hear it.

ANY STORIES THAT EMERGE FROM GRAPPLING
WITH ALMOST UNBEARABLE PAIN NOT
ONLY ENRICH OUR OWN MINDFULNESS AND
GRATITUDE BUT BOOST OUR CONFIDENCE.

One of the most effective ways to deal with past or present pain is to first talk to God about it. Get it off your chest. Don't hold it in. Tell Him how you really feel. He's big enough to handle it, and it won't scare Him, because He already knows it, anyway. When you're ready to talk to someone about it, enlist the help of a pastor, therapist, life coach, support-group, or best friend. After you've released some of that built-up pressure, you'll start to notice opportunities to use those lessons to point yourself and others toward brighter times.

To spare ourselves additional heartache, we should embrace the one-size-fits-all fact of life that joyful ups and horrific downs are parts of the thrill ride of our lives. The relief comes in knowing that, while those painful times are definitely inevitable, they certainly are not permanent.

4

FIRST IMPRESSIONS

God, please just get me out of this mess!" Why doesn't our great and benevolent God just instantly airlift us out of our pain and bad habits when we ask? I know I'm not alone in wondering about His delayed responses. At times, it can be so disheartening when those things that tempt, taunt, and haunt, stick around for so long that they become kind of like ugly pieces of furniture we can't seem to get rid of, no matter how hard we try. We have good intentions, but when we repeatedly face the pain of memories and unseemly behavior, we feel light years away from being saints or model citizens.

If we learned anything from Paul's life, as discussed in chapter 3, "Lessons Learned," I hope it is that when we feel weak, great strength is available. So maybe the reason we haven't been completely freed from our struggles and temptations is that they keep us humble. Sometimes wrongly painted as a sign of weakness, humility and dependence on God actually draw us closer to Him, and set us up to display His power.

Still, even knowing that, there's always the temptation to focus on what's not fair in our lives and fantasize about how much further along we would be if we could just get rid of certain struggles. But God is very aware that we never feel or express our need for Him as much or as emphatically as we do when we are struggling. In those times, we become painfully aware of how inadequate we are in our own strength. God absolutely loves it when we bring our issues to Him and ask for help. Then, if we let Him, He gives us personalized self-help skills which we can later use as a testimony to inspire others.

Heartbreaking

No matter what stage you're in of your journey on this planet, you've probably discovered that this life doesn't slow down, and at almost every stage, there's a good chance you will encounter heartbreak. Our hearts may ache due to broken homes, marriages, finances, friendships, or dreams. We may have suffered heartbreak at the hands of another, or we may have broken our own heart through our behavior. But now it's time to realize that what we do with those situations determines whether we develop for better or for worse. I like what Alice Walker, author of *The Color Purple*, confessed about heartache: "Every time my heart breaks, it opens a little wider." That sounds to me like a worthwhile goal to have in heartbreaking situations.

A major blockade we run into, however, is the all-too-common misconception that vulnerability is a bad thing. Many of us find it extremely difficult to face the painful truth about our weaknesses and hurts, so we often lie about it—twice. We lie to others to protect our reputations, and we lie to ourselves, because it hurts too much to look reality in the face and get real about our heartbreaks.

Refusal to face the truth of our past and accept responsibility for our actions is nothing new, of course. It's as old as the human race itself. Remember Adam and Eve's situation in the garden of Eden? They are not exactly the best role models when it comes to facing the truth. Maybe that's where the line "You can't handle the truth!" originated, long before Jack Nicholson delivered it in the movie *A Few Good Men*.

But, most likely, the reason you're reading this right now is because you *are* handling the truth—some areas of your past are still hurting you. You're also aware that you haven't seen the last of heartache; life just keeps on coming. But instead of letting those events disqualify you, and just giving up and sitting down on the sidelines, you've made the wise choice to make peace with your past. Hopefully, you're starting to see that those scars are not signs of weakness after all, and that the blockers you've been facing could actually morph into better life builders. Maybe you're starting to reverse that pain, which writer Ernest Hemingway summed up quite nicely in *A Farewell to Arms*: "The world breaks everyone and afterward many are strong at the broken places."

Training Days

You may have wondered *How did I get all these scars in the first place?* How do I know you have scars? Because I've listened to, counseled, and coached people for more than twenty years, during which I've heard a lot of recurring words and phrases that indicate scars, such as, "betrayed," "unfair," "bad luck," "taken advantage of," "stuck," "mad at myself," "feel so stupid," "don't belong," "abused," "unlovable," "depressed," "so confused," "lonely," "not enough," "addicted," and "full of rage." And these are just a few examples. Some might sound all too familiar to you.

Have you ever heard of the book *All I Really Need to Know I Learned in Kindergarten?* It's an entertaining collection of essays about the basic rules we learned way back when we started school that stick with us throughout our lives. And, according to mounting research, that book title may be truer than we realize. I don't know whether or not most people realize to what extent their childhood has influenced their adult thought and behavior patterns. As we get older, we may not understand that many of our less-than-pleasant or even all-out-destructive tendencies were reflexes formed in response to our early experiences.

AS WE GET OLDER, WE MAY NOT UNDERSTAND THAT MANY OF OUR LESS-THAN-PLEASANT OR EVEN ALL-OUT DESTRUCTIVE TENDENCIES WERE REFLEXES FORMED IN RESPONSE TO OUR EARLY EXPERIENCES.

Consider recurring incidents and issues in your life to which you've responded, "I hate it when I do that!" "That's not even my personality!" "I don't even know why I do that!" That usually means your first impressions run pretty deep. Think of using your finger to write your name in wet cement or dipping your hand in purple paint, then slapping it on a blank white canvas. First impressions are usually very noticeable and almost always memorable.

Think back to your first love or first kiss. Now, science tells us that our first impressions come in the most formative period of our lives, from birth to six years of age. We learn more during those years than we do the whole rest of our lives combined! Then along come ages seven to twelve, and then our teenage years after them. Then our twenties, thirties, forties, and so on. But the mold of our mind is pretty well cast in those foundational and developmental years—for both good and bad.

Scripture backs up this information: *"Train up a child in the way he should go: and when he is old, he will not depart from it"* (Proverbs 22:6 KJV). That is a wonderful biblical promise that many parents, including my own, have held on to when their children have gone astray. Parents have to trust that they raised their kids the best they knew how, and pray that the wayward ones will return to their training.

However, what if you were trained up in ways you should *not* go? What if some of your first impressions were of violence, drug use, alcohol abuse, bad language, fits of anger, rejection, fighting, pornography, inappropriate sexual displays, gangs, infidelity, lying, deception, disrespect, or abuse, among others? Even with good training mixed in, experiencing any of these at an impressionable age certainly leaves marks.

Fault Line

Each of us has heard, "It's all your fault" at some point in our lives, and we all know it's not a good feeling. However, in the years of discussing the impact of first impressions with individuals and groups, I've found that the majority of the blame for our unhealthy coping strategies is very often laid on our parents.

While my goal is to help people uncover the roots of unwanted behavior, we should know that the moment something clicks, allowing us to see one or more roots, it is only the beginning. That realization does not grant us permission to fix the blame squarely on Mom or Dad or anyone else who raised us, claiming, "It's not fair," and spending the rest of our lives pointing our finger at them for any and every one of our misadventures. The wisdom of Proverbs gives us fair warning about that:

> *Some people curse their father and do not thank their mother. They are pure in their own eyes, but they are filthy and unwashed. They look proudly around, casting disdainful glances. They have teeth like swords and fangs like knives.… The eye that mocks a father and despises a mother's instructions will be plucked out by ravens of the valley and eaten by vultures.* (Proverbs 30:11–14, 17)

Yikes! I would prefer to keep my eyes, wouldn't you? On this journey of self-discovery, when we recognize that our harmful habits were developed as coping strategies to help us through tough times as kids, we can't stop there. I think when most people look back on their lives, they feel a lot like country singer Kenny Chesney when he sings, "Oh, I'd done a lot of things different."[4]

SPORTING A SELF-RIGHTEOUS POUT ABOUT THE PAST, AND TALKING ABOUT WHAT COULD HAVE BEEN, DOES NOTHING BUT POISON THE PRESENT.

Sporting a self-righteous pout about the past, and talking about what could have been, does nothing but poison the present. We may or may not have had a picture-perfect upbringing, but knowing the source of our struggles can help us alleviate some of the pain that still plagues and prompts our behavior. It's clear that our background provides a treasure of building blocks for our future. No matter what we did in response to a

---

4. Bill Anderson, Dean Dillon, "A Lot of Things Different," (Sony/ATV Music Publishing LLC), 2002.

parent, sibling, grandparent, relative, neighbor, or whoever else, our past can be fuel for forming new patterns today.

The Four I's

Obviously, we all have had different experiences, but we all share a few common vulnerabilities that may have contributed to our own unique behavior. Some of the most common vulnerabilities that lead us into bad habits and unhealthy thought patterns and behaviors are what I call the four I's: ignorance, indifference, innocence, and inheritance.

Ignorance

Ignorance doesn't mean a person is dumb; it just means he or she has not learned any better. Perhaps an authority figure or another influential person in their life just didn't know any better and exposed them to, or involved them in, something unhealthy. Or perhaps that person was you!

Indifference

Indifference is a complete lack of care or an all-out disregard or intentional rebellion against authority, rules, or the status quo.

Innocence

People take advantage of another's *innocence* by crossing boundaries or violating a person in some way that makes them feel uncomfortable or completely unclean and worthless.

Inheritance

Our *inheritance* is what is passed down to us from our family members that will very often take root and produce the same fruits in us.

These four I's are gateways, or entry points, for seeds of suffering to enter into our lives and take root in our souls. These seeds may have been buried deep within us for a long time, and it wasn't until years later that they showed up unannounced to cause certain disturbances in our way of life.

The defense methods we used to cope with painful experiences through early childhood and adolescence morphed into repetitive, reflex-like behaviors, also known as habits. Those behaviors may not have been too much of a problem before, but what about now?

Habit Forming

Sometimes a strange phenomenon occurs when we don't really want to change our behavior, even when it's hurting us, because of the reward we get from it. Reward? Right. Remember when you were sick or pretended to be sick as a little kid? What happened? You very likely got to stay home from school, go back to sleep, and maybe even got served chicken noodle soup in bed! Or what about when your parents would try to get you to stop crying by offering you ice cream, a toy, or a trip to Disneyland? That was all fine and good when you were six years old, but here you are twenty-seven years later, and you're still trying to pull off stunts like that, only at this point, it may not be Mom and Dad you're trying to hustle; it's your spouse, boss, coworkers, and friends. The thing is, you've been doing it for so long, you hardly even realize you're doing it anymore. Think about the phenomenon this way:

Experiences cause thoughts.
Thoughts prompt actions.
Actions produce habits.
Habits shape lives.
Lives influence others.

Whatever you experience, you interpret it in your mind, and your thoughts produce emotions, words, and actions. These responses, if repeated, can become patterns of behavior, or habits, which are unconscious and automatic. Those habits then start to dictate the shape and quality of our lives as a whole, reflecting the truth of Aristotle's saying, "We are what we repeatedly do." It's no secret, then, that our quality of life, for better or for worse, influences everyone we come in contact with, especially those closest to us.

So to improve our responses, we may need to adjust our perceptions, starting with our immediate interpretation of past and future experiences.

It reminds me of the phrase "It is what it is." The first time I heard someone say that, I thought it was the dumbest thing I'd ever heard. *It is what it is? Of course, it is! How redundant and stupid!* But as the phrase gained popularity and I heard it more, I started thinking that it was quite a brilliant little thought, though a little adjustment was in order, because when most people said it, they sounded so defeated, kind of like, "Woe is me. It is what it is. Oh, well, there's nothing I can do about it." But I think saying "It is what it is" really is just stating that what happened, happened—boom, there it is, it's done. I've started to see it as a way to come to terms with my past; but instead of ending with a bummer, I add two words to the phrase, turning it into a question: **"It is what it is; now what?"** This moves us in the right direction toward better responses.

Too many people just come to terms with their bad habits, pain, and unwanted behavior. They learn to coexist and commiserate with them, feeling sorry for themselves, and thinking, *It is what it is.* They rationalize, make excuses, and just learn to live with it. "It is what it is" owns whatever has happened, but by adding "Now what?" we can move our minds out of the neutral gear of sadness and self-pity and into the drive gear of forward thinking. Instead of wallowing, the brain is working, thinking, *That incident is now part of my experience, so what can I do with it? What can I learn from it? Is it something I want to experience many times over or never again?*

Hard to Swallow

Sometimes, we don't want to deal with our issues because we don't want anyone else knowing about them, and just talking about them leaves a bad taste in our mouths, kind of like the bad aftertaste vegetables left in our mouths when we were growing up. I bet you can remember when you were a kid and you heard your parents say over and over, "You can't be excused from the dinner table until you eat all your vegetables." We couldn't just move them around on the plate to make it look like we had eaten them, either; we actually had to put the nasty-tasting thing into our mouths and swallow. My main battle in those days was with asparagus. There were plenty of occasions when everyone else had left the dinner table and the kitchen had been cleaned up, yet there I sat, holding my nose and choking down that gross green stuff. Funny thing is, all that "Clean your plate; it's good for you" repetition must have made my taste buds adapt, because I don't have to force myself to swallow asparagus anymore; now I actually love it.

It would be nice if swallowing our pride was as easy as swallowing vegetables. Our unwillingness to be vulnerable and open up about our background is often the very thing that keeps us buried under our struggles. Granted, there is a very large difference between swallowing vegetables and swallowing pride. A consistent intake of that good green stuff contributes to overall health, whereas nursing an overly high opinion of oneself only sets us up for a fall. The Bible states in no uncertain terms that a big ego will bring a man low, and that God opposes the overconfident. (See James 4:6.)

Of course, not all pride is bad, which is evident in qualities like dignity, self-respect, and a willingness to fight for your beliefs. But the disgusting side of pride is when we consider ourselves better than others or carry an ugly air of entitlement. Thinking we are smarter than everyone else is pride. Bragging is pride. Putting others down is pride. Pride actually makes us hide our true self. The path out of pride is spelled out in Proverbs:

> Whoever conceals their sins does not prosper, but the one who confesses and renounces them finds mercy. Blessed is the one who always trembles before God, but whoever hardens their heart falls into trouble.
>
> (Proverbs 28:13–14 NIV)

What have you been finding—mercy or trouble? Perhaps you have been unable to deal with feelings of helplessness, doubt, fear, rejection, anger, depression, or addiction, making you feel like you are in a cage. And feeling trapped and tormented for so long has resulted in unwanted actions and consequences. Maybe now you're scared of your influence on those around you. Or maybe you've been dealing with these issues for so long that you're finally ready to help yourself to some humility and get real so you can get free.

In the next few chapters, we're going to talk about what may be at the root of our bad habits and behaviors. All you have to do to be freed of your past is open up, be honest, and be willing to do whatever it takes to get better.

Are you ready?

BUILDERS AND BLOCKERS:
PRIDE VERSUS HUMILITY

To keep us trapped, the better-life blocker of *pride* makes every effort to keep us from doing a background check.

Pride

A person who is prideful has "a high or inordinate opinion of one's own…importance, merit, or superiority,"[5] exaggerated self-esteem, and haughty behavior.

To find out if pride is standing in your way, consider this brief definition and the types of behavior it may prompt. Do you see yourself in any of the following characteristics?

How Pride Looks and Acts

A person with pride is arrogant, condescending, critical, defensive, egotistical, self-centered, self-glorifying, and stubborn. They lack transparency

---

5. "pride," *Dictionary.com*, http://www.dictionary.com/browse/pride?s=t.

and have tremendous difficulty with admitting an error or making an apology. They display self-righteousness and have a condescending attitude, resisting instruction, criticism, and correction. They are consistently bragging. Their favorite topic is themselves and their favorite word is *I*. They have a tendency to take all the credit, while judging, criticizing, and comparing others.

Make It Personal

Resist the urge to think about someone else this may apply to. Be honest—this is about you. Take a moment to list any ways you see pride evident in your present behavior.

Humility

To move out of complaining and into confidence, we need the better-life builder of *humility*. Humility is "the quality or condition of being humble; modest opinion or estimate of one's own importance, rank, etc."[6] To start getting more familiar with humility, study this brief description and the following attributes of humility. Which are most attractive to you, and which do you want to develop?

How Humility Looks and Acts

A person who is humble is content, courteous, gentle, modest, meek, obliging, polite, and respectful. They regularly rank the importance of others before themselves, deflect praise to share with others, and believe strongly in teamwork. They show a willingness to admit wrong and to apologize. They are teachable, welcome critique, are genuinely interested in the opinion of others, and are open to suggestions and instruction. They don't take life too seriously but are able to laugh at themselves and take a joke.

Humility Building Material

Repetition builds skill. So take time daily to build your better life by thinking, praying, and/or saying:

---

6. "humility," *Dictionary.com*, http://www.dictionary.com/browse/humility?s=t.

Pride leads to disgrace, but with humility comes wisdom.

(Proverbs 11:2)

By humility and the fear of the Lord *are riches, and honour, and life.*

(Proverbs 22:4 kjv)

The greatest among you must be a servant.   (Matthew 23:11)

All of you, clothe yourselves with humility toward one another, because, "God opposes the proud but shows favor to the humble." Humble yourselves, therefore, under God's mighty hand, that he may lift you up in due time.   (1 Peter 5:5–6 niv)

> *"True humility is not thinking less of yourself;*
> *it is thinking of yourself less."*
> —C. S. Lewis, *Mere Christianity*

Make It Personal

Where do you need to exercise humility? Before moving on, take some time to practice the "3-R's." Ask yourself the following questions and then apply them to your life.

Reflect

1. What was the most interesting part of what I just read?
2. What will it look like when my dreams come true?
3. When have I experienced heartbreak?
4. What are some of my earliest memories? How old was I?
5. In what ways have I been trained in the way I shouldn't go?
6. Which of the four I's (ignorance, indifference, ignorance, inheritance) do I most identify with?
7. It is what it is; now what?

Release

If there is anything you need to let go of, repeat the following: "After reflecting, I see that I need to let go of _____, and I choose to release it now." Then pray,

Father, I know that when I conceal my sins, I won't prosper. So I choose to confess and renounce them so I may find your mercy. (See Proverbs 28:13.)

Renew

After releasing what's been weighing on you, what are some positive things you can commit to in the future?

Blessed is the one who always trembles before God, but whoever hardens their heart falls into trouble. (Proverbs 28:14 NIV)

PART 3

IDENTITY CRISIS:
WHAT KEEPS ME FROM
REALLY BEING MYSELF?

5

▐▛ STOLEN IDENTITY

I couldn't believe it. I had just finished my workout and walked out to my truck, only to find that my gym bag had been stolen! I had accidentally left the passenger side rear window down just enough for some lousy thief to reach in and snatch my backpack from the front seat. I was super ticked off that my favorite bag was gone due to my carelessness, but that wasn't the worst of it. What really fired me up was that my wallet had been inside of that bag.

Within a matter of minutes after this realization, I called the credit-card company to cancel my credit cards and was shocked at what I heard. The theft could not have taken place any more than an hour before, but the credit card's fraud department informed me that the culprit had already used one of my cards to buy a big lunch, fill up on gas, and shop at Walmart!

Fraud and identity theft have grown into a worldwide multibillion-dollar nightmare. Countless people have had their identities stolen, and have made horrifying discoveries of maxed-out accounts and new lines of credit opened in their names. Sometimes damage is so extensive that people have a hard time regaining control of their own name.

High Alert

Likewise, in pursuing the kind of life we've dreamed of, we have to jump the hurdle of stolen identity. The enemy of our souls is the original identity thief. The difference between him and other thieves is that he's not ultimately after our credit cards; he's after our souls. Our God-given nature and identity have always been his target. Since humans were created, his aim has been to bring us down and take us out.

The devil tried to take me out as an infant by stifling my breathing to the point that, at times, I would stop breathing and turn blue! My parents would then have to give me a few quick, firm pats on the back so I could catch my breath and start breathing again. To this day, I remain eternally grateful for the prayers of my dad, who, during the midnight hour of around-the-clock duty of keeping an eye on me, asked Jesus to heal me. Thank God, I have never had trouble breathing after that night!

It's not just our breath of life that thief is trying to steal; he's after anything he can get his claws on! I don't think we hear enough about how ruthless our enemy is and to what extent he will go to harm us with his relentless, barbaric attacks. The devil and his demons absolutely hate humanity and will go to any length to make us miserable, and, if given the chance, to kill us! There is exactly zero compassion or fairness in the evil realm of darkness. Case in point: I was only a few months old when he tried to snuff me out!

The devil's hatred fuels his burning vendetta of stealing from us, killing us, or destroying our quality of life. He attacks us as early as possible, and waits as long as needed to employ his tailor-made torment. His assaults are extremely meticulous but not usually blatant. They are more often very subtle and hidden, kind of like the black widow spider I discovered one day so very well camouflaged in the garage by my wife's car. I had never even seen a live black widow before that day. That it had built its web right where she always walks gave me the creeps, because those suckers are seriously venomous! Needless to say, it met the bottom of my shoe very quickly.

All of us have been victims of Satan's malicious attempts to murder us, destroy our property, or rob us of something of value. Even if some of the attempts have been successful, we still need not be paranoid about where the dark forces are hiding or what diabolical schemes are being planned. But we do need to be reminded to *"be alert and of sober mind [because our] enemy the devil prowls around like a roaring lion looking for someone to devour"* (1 Peter 5:8 NIV). The innovator of identity theft, that roaring lion, tries to devour the most valuable asset of all—our God-given identity.

Undercover

As sure as God desires that each of us find joy in each chapter of our story and live happily ever after, the devil is bent on destroying us. He has a horde of horror stories he wants to include in our lives. He delivers the beat-downs and blowups from hell with a sinister resolve designed to frighten, discourage, and overwhelm anyone determined to enjoy life. Each incident can dim the light in our eyes, leaving us looking and feeling tired, stifled, and nearly unrecognizable. We may start to wonder who we are, and what became of the people we used to be.

By attacking our identity, Satan mercilessly fires away at our quality of life, as if a giant bull's-eye were painted on our self-image. He aims to damage our soul and body as early, as often, and as deeply as possible, so that our wounds affect us in every stage of our lives from childhood through adolescence and into adulthood. Two tools he commonly uses with incredible effectiveness are rejection and abandonment.

BY ATTACKING OUR IDENTITY, SATAN MERCILESSLY FIRES AWAY AT OUR QUALITY OF LIFE, AS IF A GIANT BULL'S-EYE WERE PAINTED ON OUR SELF-IMAGE.

Reject means to "discard as useless or unsatisfactory...to cast out or off."[7] It is to dishonor, turn down, or refuse a person love. A person who is rejected is excluded and given the cold shoulder, which can feel like a slap

---

7. "reject," *Dictionary.com*, http://www.dictionary.com/browse/abandon?s=t.

in the face. *Abandon* means "to forsake utterly; desert...leave."[8] Both of these tragic weapons are closely related in that they both involve a lack of love.

No matter where people come from or where they end up, nobody on this planet can escape the heinous feeling of being excluded or deserted or both. I know of a world-famous rock star whose dad left him when he was very young. This star spent the rest of his childhood being shipped off to live with relatives every time his mom met a new man. He talked about how his experiences introduced and intimately acquainted him with abandonment in a way that left him feeling unlovable, and his wounds festered into all sorts of bad things.

That kind of stuff is heavy—especially for children. We all want to be loved and accepted, and at no time in life is that need more evident than during those developmental years. Though, whenever we experience a lack of love, whether as a child or as an adult, we can start to lose our true identity, or have it stolen from us, and we develop coping methods to help control something we can't control. Hiding in a closet; trying to be perfect; escaping into a fantasy world; using drugs or alcohol, and so forth, slowly become habits, or an alternative to expressing true feelings of mistreatment and helplessness. We just do the best we can to survive by denying needs and burying feelings.

WHENEVER WE EXPERIENCE A LACK OF LOVE,
WHETHER AS A CHILD OR AS AN ADULT,
WE CAN START TO LOSE OUR TRUE IDENTITY,
OR HAVE IT STOLEN FROM US, AND WE
DEVELOP COPING METHODS TO HELP CONTROL
SOMETHING WE CAN'T CONTROL.

If we are not careful or are never taught any different, those methods may begin to mask our identity. Different incidents and accidents can produce layers and labels that inadvertently send our true identity into hiding.

---

8. "abandon," *Dictionary.com*, http://www.dictionary.com/browse/abandon?s=t.

Everybody Hurts

At one time or another, we all have been rejected, and quite frequently, we end up feeling like rejects trying to relate to other rejected or abandoned people, which causes all sorts of personal problems and relationship roadblocks. When one rejected person gets into a relationship with another rejected person, likely there will be more than just roadblocks—there will be potholes, land mines, and fireworks, too. And that type of track record often results in us being tagged with another suffocating label: "Does not play well with others." It's a vicious cycle; when we have a hard time getting along with other people, it's more than likely because we have a hard time even liking ourselves. We drain a lot of our mental energy feeling bad for ourselves, and then withdraw and isolate ourselves, which depresses us even more.

Then there are the times when we absolutely *have* to be around people, so we begrudgingly go somewhere and either act fake or wear our frustration or sadness on our sleeves until we end up spilling our bad mood onto somebody else. Afterward, a confrontation or incident may ensue, prompting us to run away and berate ourselves even more. At this point, we retreat further into isolation or into an alternate identity.

We adopt alternate identities usually due to fear. Treated like we had no value, or deserted altogether some time in our past, we fear being authentic. Uncertain of how others will respond to us, fear can then mask some sides of our personality almost permanently. So many people try to fit in to what our society labels as normal or average, and any hint of individuality gets squashed for fear of standing out.

Courageous individuality definitely stands out, and for all the right reasons. I witnessed a good example of this on a recent trip to the gym. As I was working out, I heard, "Just five more! You're looking good! Four! Come on now! Three! You can do it! Two! Make this last one count! Great job!" The exuberant commands were coming from the aerobics room. When I walked by the glass wall on my way to the water fountain, I noticed that the instructor looked a bit more full-figured than most other aerobics trainers I had encountered. She looked more like someone who had just started taking the class than someone who would be teaching it.

As I continued my workout, I found myself thinking about the bravery that woman must have had to step out to lead aerobics. Like most any other human being, she probably had reservations about it and had to overcome her own fears of doing something new. Like any of us, she probably felt self-conscious about getting up in front of people, no matter her physique. She's a perfect example of what happens when we look fear in the face and stare it down—we *lead*.

Any honest man who has gone on to success in his field will tell you that before he ended up leading anything, he had to face his fears. It doesn't matter if the field is fitness, business, parenting, or so forth. In order to advance, some people push past fear, while others just do whatever it is they want or need to do, even though they still feel very much afraid.

Fear Factors

Rejected or abandoned growing up, most of us responded in fear or hurt and started to believe that it was all our fault. Then with that mistaken notion, feeling as if the weight of the world had landed on our shoulders, we took on responsibilities that were never ours in the first place. Perhaps we thought it was our fault that our parents were fighting, so we tried to distract them by making them laugh, being a model student, or covering up the addiction or bad behavior of one parent so the other wouldn't find out and leave for good.

What most of us never realize about taking on those unassigned responsibilities is that over time, they become a part of our personality. Although not all negative, the reflexes we developed for protection tend to separate us from our true nature, from others, and from God. At times, we might take on another persona completely—somebody we don't even recognize—with behaviors and a personality so different from who we started out to be initially. Rejection or abandonment can make us so disgusted with ourselves that we completely stifle our true personality.

I've had the privilege of working with some famous faces from the world of sports and entertainment over the years, and whenever I think of the effects of rejection, one face in particular comes to mind. But in this case, it's not about *his* response to rejection; it's about mine.

Anytime I went anywhere with this famous guy, people would rush over to get his autograph or a picture with him. It was usually quite a scene. As interesting as it was to be around that type of attention, shortly into the journey of helping him on his path to a better life, I got a strange vibe—I felt like he didn't like me. I discussed it with a friend who was also helping him, and he said that he felt the same thing—like this "Mr. Everything" actor didn't like either of us, even though we both were doing our best to help him.

So you know what happened? Even though my friend and I continued to be around and offer help to this man, I kept thinking, *Shoot! I don't care who he is. If he doesn't like me, I don't like him, either!* The problem with that type of thinking and behavior is that it's not me. I like people. I always have. I just love being around people, and I truly have a passion for helping them. So for me to even consider not liking someone was unnatural. But that's what rejection does to us. When we feel unappreciated or disrespected, we act like people we are not.

Later I realized that our famous friend was actually not rejecting us because he didn't like us. He was just extremely guarded. He had been in the public eye for a long time, and everywhere he went, somebody wanted something from him. He just hadn't known me well enough to let his guard down. I felt pretty dumb after realizing that the rejection all had been in my head. Fear of rejection, real or perceived, really can make us do dumb things!

Our abilities are developed and confidence is produced when we know our identity. If we don't know our identity, we will consistently wonder, *What's wrong with me?*—which produces more and more fear.

The fear that comes with rejection and/or abandonment is often masked by a more socially acceptable term we hear or say every day—*worry.* I mean, these days it's almost as if we're being completely irresponsible if we're not worrying about something, right? No matter how it is labeled or even rationalized away, anxiety is just too costly. Statistics say that it costs each person in the United States over $1500 a year to treat all the anxiety-related mental issues in the country! And there's no way to estimate the toll it takes on our careers, relationships, bodies, and spirits. We need to uncover our true identity so we can take our lives back!

6

BE TRUE TO YOU

Y ou're going to hell!"

No. Not you. A friend of mine heard those words from his youth leader at the church he attended growing up. Apparently, the ultimate sin that had been deemed worthy of eternal condemnation and damnation was that my friend had begun to realize his love for music, for he started playing guitar and growing out his hair. Usually, when a young person develops a passionate desire for something, it is a happy occasion. It generally is an indicator of talents and traits that will enhance that person's personality and contribute to his or her identity. But in this case, the supposedly well-meaning but narrow-minded youth leader made it clear that, in his mind, rock and roll could not possibly coexist with God. Not long after that incident, the long-haired teenage rock 'n' roller decided that church and God were not for him.

After he told me this story, I told him that I had a similar experience with an overly religious youth pastor who made fun of my long hair and told me that any song that didn't say "Jesus" in it was the devil's music. That added serious fuel to my teenage angst and had made me want to stay away from church too.

A few years after, however, at the age of nineteen, I admitted what I had known all along, that God's plans were better for me than my own. So I asked God to let me know Him and relate to Him in a way that didn't involve being a religious, holier-than-thou person. I did not want, nor did I think I could stomach, a judgmental attitude like the one I had seen in legalistic youth pastors and others. After a heartfelt prayer, admitting that I was a sinner and inviting Christ into my life, I was elated at how quickly I discovered the outlandishly liberating difference between choosing a relationship with God and choosing religion.

For Identification Purposes

History has proven the traditions and standards of organized religion to be extremely helpful in guiding people and helping them find their divinely inspired identity in Christ. But unless religion is guided by what Jesus proclaimed in Matthew 22 to be the greatest commandment of all—to love God and others as we do ourselves—it can easily be abused and swung around like a wrecking ball. On the other hand, the guidelines of the law in a relationship with our Creator should produce in us creativity, along with an anchor of devotion, a sense of security, and the freedom to express ourselves, to love, and to be loved.

Even though my friend is still unsure of where he stands with God, I am grateful for the opportunities we've had to discuss our experiences. And it is obvious God has a great sense of humor because those conversations took place on a bus—a *tour bus*. I was serving as The Better Life Coach, and he was the guitarist for a multiplatinum rock-and-roll band! Yes, that is definitely one of those convincing "God shots" that reveals how knowing God is always better than knowing the rules.

Not long after I had started experiencing the night-and-day difference between religion and freedom, I felt that the God I was getting to know as a Person asked me if I would represent Him as a minister. In my limited understanding, I knew that if I were to say yes, I would have to change completely everything about myself to fit into the mold of ministry. I figured it meant I would have to lock myself away from the rest of society like a monk on a mountain, or that I would have to slick my hair back and wear a suit and tie all the time. I might even have to start speaking in that strange-sounding kind of preacher voice.

The thing is, I had great role models growing up; my dad, grandpa, and great-grandpa were ministers nothing like what I just described. They had pioneered churches and founded Bible colleges, risked their lives doing missionary work in hostile foreign territory, and helped change literally thousands upon thousands of lives. But in the shadow of these amazing men, I was still so painfully aware of my own limitations and the glaring contrasts between me and other ministers that it caused me some serious apprehension.

That's when the beauty of communicating and being in a relationship with God became more apparent to me. My image of an overlord type of figure dictating harsh rules was fading fast, as I felt God becoming more like a close friend than I had ever known was possible. That Friend began revealing to me, from the inside out, that He had never intended for me to take on the look, personality, methods, or speaking style of another man. I'll never forget the sensation of freedom, validation, and excitement that began bubbling up inside as He reminded me over and over again, "I'm not asking you to be like your dad, grandpa, or great-grandpa. I want you to be you." The revelation that God gives us each unique identities for a reason finally convinced me. "Yes. I'll do it," I said.

Insecurity Guard

Now as I look back on that decision, decades later, I am even more grateful I said yes to the One who wants me to be me. I have found it not just sad but also immensely inspiring that so many people who are near death have wished that they would have expressed more of their feelings. Far too many have said that if they had it to do over again, they would live their life, not trying to please others or be who others wanted them to be, but rather, paying much more attention to their own heart's desires and spending their days being true to themselves. The sad part is that so many have reached death's doorstep by the time they realize the value of self-expression. But remember what we learned in chapter 3, "Lessons Learned"? Life is full of lessons. How inspiring to be able to learn from the experiences of others, so we can start improving the quality of our still very-much-alive experiences right away.

FAR TOO MANY HAVE SAID THAT IF THEY HAD IT TO DO OVER AGAIN, THEY WOULD LIVE THEIR LIFE, NOT TRYING TO PLEASE OTHERS OR BE WHO OTHERS WANTED THEM TO BE, BUT RATHER, PAYING MUCH MORE ATTENTION TO THEIR OWN HEART'S DESIRES AND SPENDING THEIR DAYS BEING TRUE TO THEMSELVES.

"How am I supposed to do that?" you may ask. "You don't know all the hell I've had to go through in my life." You're right. I don't know any of those details. But I do know that enduring hardships—such as a physical or learning disability, constant comparisons, a nasty betrayal, or any other painful, devaluing experiences—chips away at who we are, eroding our willingness to open up to people. Our identity is breached, allowing insecurity to set up shop and distribute all sorts of fears. Insecure, we try to walk, talk, or act differently, maybe even wear certain clothing to camouflage or attract attention. Afraid to be embarrassed again, we make all kinds of adjustments in the way we do things, so maybe, just maybe, we'll measure up to what we've been compared to over and over again. And, of course, due to our ever-expanding fear of betrayal, we never even consider getting close to anyone. We tell ourselves, "Well, it is just safer to stay at home, away from people, and watch TV."

But remember, a little goes a long way. A good place to start is simply adjusting your outlook. Take, for instance, a guy I know who responds to the question "How's it going?" with, "Well, we're doing the best we can with what we've got!" I loved that answer the first time I heard it, and I have been doing my best to adopt his mind-set ever since. Over time, it has done wonders in helping me handle life with a pretty consistent demeanor, no matter what measure of good, bad, or ugly lands on my doorstep. I've also learned that science and research actually show the benefits of that kind of thinking. Saying "This too shall pass," "No worries," or "Everything will be alright," even in the face of unfavorable conditions, is incredibly helpful, because that type of talk can literally train our brains to form new connections, replacing the old doom-and-gloom, woe-is-me mentality.

I bet you can do the best you can with what you've got, too! Oh, anyone could do less with what he has, but nobody can do better than his best. Maybe it will positively influence your identity, like it has mine. You never know, something as simple as a new way of talking can noticeably improve the way you face challenges over time. This is very helpful because, if you're like me, you have realized that there is no shortage of challenges in this life!

Bullied

In middle school, I had one of those challenging experiences that many children have growing up: I was picked on by a bully. He was bigger than most of my friends, and he liked to play the tough guy by calling people names and pushing around anyone who would let him.

I let him. I had been taught not to fight. So I was intimidated by his tactics of pretending like he was going to punch me and bumping me really hard with his shoulder as he passed by in the hallway. After I flinched or just took whatever he dished out, he would usually give me a menacing look or rattle off some familiar line used by most bullies—"You gonna do something about it?"

After a little while, this harassment got inside my head and made me a bit skittish. Back then, there was no anti-bullying movement that told me how valuable I was, so I started to feel like a weakling, all the while knowing I wasn't really weak. I just tried to do the right thing by not fighting back, and I started trying to avoid him as best I could. I was no king of the school by any stretch of the imagination, but I hated feeling scared to walk through the halls, in the cafeteria, and anywhere I went on school property. I was always looking over my shoulder. The insecurity was uncomfortable and completely unnatural for me.

To compound the problem, as the semester progressed, I started feeling uncomfortable outside of school, too. I was edgy on the bus, at any extracurricular activities, and even at home. Sometimes I would go to bed thinking about some run-in with the bully I had endured that day, and wake up the next morning dreading what embarrassing moment might be in store for me *that* day. At times, I would feel nauseated and contemplate the old trick of faking sickness so I could have a break from the problem. Finally, one night, I told my dad about what was going on and how not fighting back was making me feel more and more like a wimp.

His response changed everything. He said, "Son, you're right. I'm proud of you. It's true that you should not go around starting fights, but if someone starts a fight with you, you finish it!" I couldn't believe my ears! I felt like I had just been set free from torture! My days of walking scared were over.

I woke up early the next morning feeling entirely different than I had in previous weeks. I was actually excited to go to school that day. Sure enough, as I was about to pass that bully in the hallway between classes, he walked toward me and bumped my shoulder as he had done so many times. Aware of my newfound freedom to fight back, I whipped around and shoved him so hard, he stumbled awkwardly and nearly fell over! As he caught his balance, he looked at me surprised, and I stared back at him with raised eyebrows and a confident smirk, as if to say, "You gonna do something about it?"

I never had any trouble with him again.

Unmasked

We all have been bullied in one way or another. Whether you've thought about it this way or not, fear is a bully. Maybe you weren't called names or pushed around in the school hallway, but your identity has taken a beating from an obsession with imagining worst-case scenarios. You might be tormented by discouragement or be caught in the crippling fear of what other people think of you. The original identity thief does not dispatch some spooky boogeyman to sabotage us; he sends real demons, and too many people fight them every day and night in silent agony. The behaviors we adopt when terrorized by anxiety are not natural. They keep our identities under wraps, our lives marked by masquerading stage performances.

THE BEHAVIORS WE ADOPT WHEN TERRORIZED BY ANXIETY ARE NOT NATURAL. THEY KEEP OUR IDENTITIES UNDER WRAPS, OUR LIVES MARKED BY MASQUERADING STAGE PERFORMANCES.

Remember wearing a mask on Halloween as a kid? I sure do. I remember them being uncomfortable—hot, sweaty, and heavy, it was difficult to see or even breathe. We went through all that hassle, but at least we got rewarded with bags of candy! But these days, we wear masks when there's no reward, only discomfort. Fear masks us with a red clown noses to make people laugh in hopes they don't see our sadness. Fear burdens us with black-bandit eye masks to make us look tough instead of sensitive. Fear fits us with phantom masks to hide certain parts of ourselves. Fear covers us with shiny, sparkling masks to make us appear like goody-goodies. Fear may even issue us superhero costumes, in which we take on the role of saving everybody but ourselves.

If you've been suffocating under a bunch of roles you really hate to play, it's time to confront the fear bully. Like my dad told me, "If someone starts a fight with you, you finish it!" Our Father in heaven knew we would encounter heavyweight bouts of anxiousness, so He detailed a challenge for us in the many variations of the words *"Do not fear"* (see, for example, Isaiah 35:4) throughout the Bible.

Come Out, Wherever You Are

It's time to stop covering up who you really are. Stop letting what you want always get swept under layers of fear. Come on! Fight! Come out, come out, wherever you are! The sooner you reveal the real you, the sooner you can start enjoying the life you were meant to live! Jesus gave us permission to handle absolutely any infringement on our true nature when He said, *"I have given you authority over all the power of the enemy, and you can walk among snakes and scorpions and crush them. Nothing will injure you"* (Luke 10:19). That authority gives you and me the power to unmask ourselves by fighting intimidation. We don't have to back down or run in fear ever again. Courage is a much better look for us.

To jump-start your courage, confess the following seven statements about who you are when you're in a relationship with God. Get used to seeing and saying them to spark the real you. Confess one each day of the week to help reveal your true identity.

- "I am a child of God." (See John 1:12.)

- "I am meant for a better life." (See John 10:10.)

- "I am in Christ. Apart from Him, I can do nothing." (See John 15:5.)

- "I am made alive by the same Spirit that raised Christ." (See Romans 8:11.)

- "I am a new person. Old things are over; now is new." (See 2 Corinthians 5:17.)

- "I am led by God's Spirit; I don't give in to my flesh." (See Galatians 5:16.)

- "I am God's work of art, created to do good works." (See Ephesians 2:10.)

BUILDERS AND BLOCKERS:
FEAR VERSUS COURAGE

To mask our true identity, the better-life blocker of *fear* tries to invade every possible area of our lives, so we are almost always apprehensive about being ourselves.

Fear

Fear is "a distressing emotion aroused by impending danger, evil, pain, etc., whether the threat is real or imagined…something that causes feelings of dread or apprehension."[9] To find out if fear has too much of an influence on you, consider this brief definition and the following behaviors it may cause in us. Do you see any of the following characteristics in yourself?

How Fear Looks and Acts

A person who is fearful is angst-ridden, cowardly, jittery, stressed, timid, tormented, and insecure. They have an overactive imagination about

---

9. "fear," *Dictionary.com*, http://www.dictionary.com/browse/fear?s=t.

worst-case scenarios, limiting new ventures, relationships, risk-taking, or using personal gifts and talents. They are easily intimidated, or, to compensate, overly intimidating to others. They are often discouraged, feel inadequate, can't say no, and freeze up. They are obsessive about the past; anxious about the future; frequently sick; indecisive; and tormented by nightmares, insomnia, depression, and loneliness. They have panic attacks and irrationally avoid certain places or things due to phobias of specific objects, activities, or situations; for example, they may fear spiders, heights, small spaces, confrontations, or intimacy. They may isolate themselves and become overprotective of children, spouse, possessions, and positions.

Make It Personal

Resist the urge to think about someone else this may apply to. Be honest—this is about you. Take a moment to list any ways you see fear evident in your present behavior.

Courage

If you've ever had an identity crisis, you need the better-life builder of *courage*, "the quality of mind or spirit that enables a person to face difficulty, danger, pain, etc., without fear; bravery"[10]

To understand courage, study this brief definition and the following example of how it looks to be courageous. Which of the following characteristics would look good on you?

How Courage Looks and Acts

A person who is courageous is adventurous, brave, cool, gritty, gutsy, lionhearted, resolute, tenacious, and valiant. They have determination in the face of challenging tasks and confrontations. They display confidence and a willingness to take risks while others play it safe. They are unafraid to stand alone, remain steadfast and bold in convictions when others bow to pressure or keep the status quo. They appear calm in turbulent times, take initiative, and remain selfless in relationships and interaction.

10. "courage," *Dictionary.com*, http://www.dictionary.com/browse/courage.

Courage Building Material

Repetition builds skill. So take time daily to build your better life by thinking, praying, and/or saying:

Be strong and courageous! Do not be afraid or discouraged. For the LORD *your God is with you wherever you go.* (Joshua 1:9)

For God hath not given us the spirit of fear; but of power, and of love, and of a sound mind. (2 Timothy 1:7 KJV)

"Courage is resistance to fear, mastery of fear, not absence of fear."
—Mark Twain, *Pudd'nhead Wilson*

"Courage is what it takes to stand up and speak; courage is also what it takes to sit down and listen."
—Winston Churchill

Make It Personal

What are you facing that requires courage? Before moving on, take some time to practice the "3-R's" by asking yourself the following questions and then applying them to your life.

Reflect

1. What stood out to me in this chapter on identity?
2. Fear often makes us do some unnatural things. What are some unnatural things I do out of fear?
3. What people in my life make me feel like I can't be myself?
4. When was the last time I felt really comfortable in my own skin?
5. What do I do that makes me uncomfortable? Where and with whom?

6. How does it feel to totally be myself?

Release

If there is anything you need to let go of, repeat the following: "After reflecting, I see that I need to let go of _____, and I choose to release it now." Then pray this prayer:

> Heavenly Father, I cast my burden of fear on You. I release the weight of it now, and thank You for sustaining me and not allowing me to slip, fall, or fail. (See Psalm 55:22.)

Renew

After releasing all fear and identity thieves, what are some ways you can employ the better-life builder of courage in the future?

> *Therefore, if anyone is in Christ, he is a new creation; old things have passed away; behold, all things have become new.*
>
> (2 Corinthians 5:17 NKJV)

To reveal even more of the real you, here is just a partial list of what Scripture says about our God-given identity. Read, pray, and proclaim these truths.

What is true of Jesus is true of me:

+   I am the salt of the earth and the light of the world. (See Matthew 5:13–14.)

+   I am a child of God. (See John 1:12.)

+   I am meant for a better life. (See John 10:10.)

+   I am in Christ. Apart from Him, I can do nothing. (See John 15:5.)

+   I am Christ's friend, and His life flows through me. (See John 15:15.)

+   I am chosen by Christ to bear fruit. (See John 15:16.)

+   I am Christ's witness, sent to tell everyone about Him. (See Acts 1:8.)

- I am made alive by the same Spirit that raised Christ. (See Romans 8:11.)
- I am a child of God; I call Him my Father. (See Romans 8:14 –15.)
- I am a coheir with Christ, inheriting His glory. (See Romans 8:17.)
- I am a temple of God. His Spirit lives in me. (See 1 Corinthians 3:16.)
- I am joined to the Lord, one in spirit with Him. (See 1 Corinthians 6:17.)
- I am part of Christ's body. (See 1 Corinthians 12:27.)
- I am a new me. The old is over; new is now. (See 2 Corinthians 5:17.)
- I am reconciled with God, helping others find peace. (See 2 Corinthians 5:18.)
- I am a child of God, one with others in His family. (See Galatians 3:26, 28.)
- I am God's child and will receive an inheritance. (See Galatians 4:6–7.)
- I am called to live in freedom. (See Galatians 5:13.)
- I am led by God's Spirit; I don't give in to my flesh. (See Galatians 5:16.)
- I am a saint, a holy person. (See Ephesians 1:1.)
- I am a citizen of heaven, seated in the heavenly realms above evil. (See Ephesians 2:6.)
- I am God's work of art, created to do His good work. (See Ephesians 2:10.)
- I am righteous and holy. (See Ephesians 4:24.)
- I am hidden with Christ in God. (See Colossians 3:3.)
- I am chosen of God, holy and dearly loved. (See Colossians 3:12.)
- I am a child of light, not of darkness. (See 1 Thessalonians 5:5.)
- I am chosen to share in God's heavenly calling. (See Hebrews 3:1.)

+ I am in this with Christ; I share in His life. (See Hebrews 3:14.)

+ I am one of God's living stones. (See 1 Peter 2:5.)

+ I am a member of a chosen race, a royal priesthood. (See 1 Peter 2:9.)

+ I am a visitor to this temporary world. (See 1 Peter 2:11.)

+ I am an enemy of the devil. (See 1 Peter 5:8.)

+ I am God's child; I'll be like Christ when He returns. (See 1 John 3:1–2.)

+ I am born again in Christ, and the devil cannot touch me. (See 1 John 5:18.)

PART 4

WHERE IS THE LOVE?:
WHY CAN'T I FIND,
OR EVEN DEFINE, LOVE?

7

▛ MISSED CONNECTION

Every year, my wife and I make it a priority to go on several outings with friends or family. Sometimes, it's just for a day or two with another couple; and other times, if possible, I go on a guy's trip and she goes on a girl's trip. I've always found the guy's trips, most likely scheduled around a sporting event or two, to be very memorable experiences. For me, these trips are never really as much about visiting new ballparks, even though one of my life goals is to visit every NFL and MLB stadium, as it is about just spending time with one or more of my best buddies. Long after the trips are over, they leave a lasting impression. I have been truly blessed with the gift of enduring relationships that make day-to-day life very fulfilling.

Relationships can be one of the most rewarding aspects of our lives. Sharing the great and not-so-great experiences of life with another person or group of people adds another level of enjoyment and support, which is missing for those who go it alone. You could be having the most amazing experience of a lifetime, but unless there's someone there to take in all the sights and sensations with you, it can seem flat. By the same token, you could be going through hell and high water, but it's easier with someone there to share the load. If you have to face dark times all alone, hopelessness tends to creep in. Life's not good when you're disconnected.

What Is Love?

One of the facts of life is that we were created for connection. In the beginning, after God created the heavens and the earth, the sun and the moon, the land and sea, and the plants and the animals, He saw that it was good, but He wanted to share it with someone. So He decided to create human beings for that very purpose—to *share* life.

Jesus was asked by a bunch of crafty religious leaders, "*Which is the most important commandment…?*" (Matthew 22:36). Seeing right through their efforts to trick Him into approving their misguided, rule-based view of pleasing God, Jesus responded,

> "*You must love the* LORD *your God with all your heart, all your soul, and all your mind." This is the first and greatest commandment. A second is equally important: "Love your neighbor as yourself." The entire law and all the demands of the prophets are based on these two commandments.*   (Matthew 22:37–40)

Love? That's it? Is it really that simple? Well, most of us have discovered by now that to love and to be loved are definitely not simple. They are very complex and powerful. Something strong enough to build bridges or move mountains is not to be taken lightly, which is precisely why rejection and abandonment make such deep and lasting impressions on us. Every refusal or denial of love since the time we were conceived raises questions about our identity. Those ordeals and nagging questions tend to eat away at our self-image, giving us an unhealthy view of ourselves, which can be our biggest barrier to experiencing true love. Furthermore, when we are tossed aside, turned down, or forsaken, we get the clear message that love is conditional, that we have to *earn* it somehow. But at its core, pure, unadulterated love is *unconditional*.

Every time we attempt to earn love, our self-image gets a little more distorted.

Every one of us has dealt with a lack of love from time to time (or a bunch of times), and we all have developed coping mechanisms. What are coping mechanisms? They are whatever we started doing to help deal with whatever made us feel helpless, unwanted, or unlovable. Coping mechanisms, more often than not, are developed when a person is either too young to know what he is doing or just too numb to care. Lack of love probably made us feel like damaged goods, and we wanted someone, something—anything to make us feel better. Having been devalued or deserted, some of us are still genuinely wondering, *What is love?* Or perhaps we haven't even noticed the lack of love shown to us. Over time, our coping mechanisms start to smother our identity.

EVERY TIME WE ATTEMPT TO EARN LOVE, OUR SELF-IMAGE GETS A LITTLE MORE DISTORTED.

The Roots

The roots of rejection or abandonment in our life determine the fruit in our life. And by "fruit," I am talking about the type of things that are produced by the way we spend our time and energy. So if we are seeing fruits that we don't like, such as bad habits and compulsive thoughts or behavior, unless we want to continue inflicting pain on ourselves and others, perhaps we should examine our roots.

Not everybody gets excited when the talk turns to personal roots, though, because getting to the roots requires some digging, and digging can be dirty. Some might say, "Well, yes, I've heard of stuff like this before, and I've dealt with all of it already." I am familiar with apprehension that arises when dealing with developmental issues, because I used to be apprehensive about it myself, and I've had people who want to skip out of coaching sessions due to it. One of my strengths is helping people discover what it is from their past that plagues their present, but some people just get scared about what might be dug up. Some just flat out refuse to get their hands dirty, and others figure that this getting to the root needs to happen only to other people, and that they're the exception.

My response to that line of thinking is that no matter how good of a handle you may have on life right now—surprise! Life is full of surprises—some good, some bad—and as long as we're alive, incidents and accidents will keep happening. So we have to learn and relearn, and then learn again, how to handle life as it unfolds.

Below are some incidents that may have caused rejection or abandonment to take root in your life. As you read through this list, take time to prayerfully consider if any, or possibly several, of them apply to you. Go ahead—be honest and circle all that apply.

Unwanted pregnancy

Abortion

Birth defects

Physical disabilities

Comparison

Adoption

Abuse

Neglect

Taunting/teasing

Death of a parent or loved one

Poverty

Violence

Divorce of parents

A latchkey childhood

Betrayal by a friend, loved one, or business partner

Adultery or divorce

Blended family

Peer pressure

Ancestors

If any of these have caused rejection or abandonment in your life, the odds are that you've also experienced some of the following common but unhealthy behavior patterns in response to insufficient love. As with the incidents above, don't rush through this list. Take time to identify and circle the toxic emotions and destructive thought/behavior patterns that apply to you.

Rebellion

Self-pity

Bitterness

Hatred of others

Self-hatred

Anger

Rejection of God and others	Nagging loneliness
Escapism	Hypersensitivity
Overthinking	Self-mutilation
Extreme competition	Chronic guilt
Defensiveness	Panic attacks
Distrust	Lingering grief
Perfectionism	Self-sabotage
Fear	High-risk behaviors
Health issues	Fear of intimacy
Poverty	Inability to form lasting relationships
Poor self-image	
Hopelessness	Isolation
Disrespect	Feelings of neglect or worthlessness
Eating disorders	Substance abuse
Violence	Addiction
Depression	Inability to give or receive love

Please understand that my intention in bringing up these horrendous experiences is not to add insult to injury, but to help identify the sources of your pain, as separate from your true identity. I hope to help you see them as they are—past events—instead of permanent personality traits that define you.

You may have been hurt; tortured; molested; used; degraded; physically, verbally, sexually, or emotionally abused; threatened; harassed; beaten; raped; assaulted; ignored; neglected; cheated on; lied to; or had some other horrific thing happen to you. So often these traumatic experiences, no matter the stage of life in which they occur, produce in us an underlying frustration, unhappiness, or dissatisfaction.

I once listened to a former porn star describe that underlying frustration as she poured out her heart about the pain she had endured as a child due to her father's unimaginably cruel treatment of her. She talked about how the nagging guilt and feelings of worthlessness continued to plague her throughout her teenage years and into her adult life. Those feelings were so strong that immediately after she had endured a nightmarish gang rape as a teenager and had been dumped on the side of the road, her dominant thought was, *What am I going to tell my dad?* To keep him from getting upset and taking it out on her, she decided to bury the real story of the savage rape down inside her and tell him instead that she had been beaten up by some girls.

This woman, who had been so used and degraded for most of her life, demonstrated by her former profession and patterns of risky behavior, as well as obsessive and compulsive actions, that all she was really trying to do was find the love and attention she craved. Looking much older than forty years, she shared that despite her success, she always felt dissatisfied, and that almost every time she got excited about something good that was about to happen, she would somehow sabotage it and once again become depressed. Her inability to sustain any long-term relationship hasn't helped her mind-set, either; instead, it usually prompts bouts of isolation and substance abuse. This sad, sick cycle all began with a major root cause being the lack of love.

Undecided

Once we start digging to discover roots and making peace with our past, we must not regret things we did not choose. We would have never chosen the negative situations that have occurred in our lives; we truly were just victims of circumstance.

Remember reading about the four I's in chapter 4, "First Impressions"? Ignorance, innocence, and inheritance may have been involved in situations we did not decide (indifference is generally decided). We may have been ignorant of the circumstances, we may have been innocent, or we may have simply inherited certain undesirable traits, passed down through the family tree. But whatever the case, if we've been beating ourselves up over something that was involuntarily inserted into our lives, something we did not decide to include, it is no use continuing to do so. Why not decide to stop regretting it right now? Stop letting someone else's action or lack of action keep your mind all tied up with wishful thinking about the past. Take your power back!

Trouble doesn't have to bury us. As a matter of fact, no matter what form it takes or where it comes from, trouble can transform us. Every crisis demonstrates and creates character. The type of character that's created, however, is entirely up to us.

For instance, I saw an afternoon talk-show panel discuss how batteries might produce harmful effects on people and the environment. The host asked the main guest what she wanted to do about the problem, and she described her extensive plan to push for battery reform laws at the local, state, and federal levels.

EVERY CRISIS DEMONSTRATES AND CREATES CHARACTER. THE TYPE OF CHARACTER THAT'S CREATED, HOWEVER, IS ENTIRELY UP TO US.

Admittedly, my knowledge on the harmful effects of batteries is minimal, but I do strongly believe in standing up for what you believe in. I do know that pushing for someone else to produce change is not always the answer. It seems to me that if I am pushing others to make the changes I feel need to be made, I am setting myself up to blame anyone but myself if things don't go the way I want them to go.

Think about it, if our boss implements a new work policy that we don't like, would our best plan of action be to force him to rework it to accommodate us? If there is an issue in one of our relationships, should we try to change the other person's behavior? What if we aren't in shape; should we point our finger at the fast-food industry? Now, don't get me wrong: if we can act to bring resolution to an issue, by all means, we need to act. But if we're spending brain power and energy on efforts beyond our control, now is a good time to assess whether or not we're just spinning our wheels and getting dirtier and more bogged down in the muck of frustration. The only people on this planet we truly have any control over is ourselves. So if we want to build a better life, we must grasp the concept "If it is to be, it is up to me."

Wits' End

"Ok. So it's up to me. But what if I don't know what to do? What if I feel like I'm at my wits' end?" Ever been there? I'm sure we all have felt that gnawing sensation of helplessness at least once. Actually, in our do-it-yourself culture, that sinking feeling of having exhausted every effort is quite common. But suppose several things happen all at once, leaving us feeling overwhelmed and on the edge of hopelessness. What do we do then?

One of the most effective ways to learn and grow is to follow the example of those who have been in similar situations but who have made it through. The Bible tells us a story of frustrated souls who found the right path of triumph over hopelessness:

> *They were at their wits' end. Then they cried out to the* Lord *in their trouble, and he brought them out of their distress. He stilled the storm to a whisper; the waves of the sea were hushed. They were glad when it grew calm, and he guided them to their desired haven.*
>
> (Psalm 107:27–30 NIV)

As we journey through our day-to-day lives, it is not really a question of *if* we will face wits'-end situations but *how* we will respond to them when they occur. From this Scripture, we see that calling out to God to get involved in our dilemmas can pave the way out of despair and into life. Knowing that our help comes from above can be just the right boost when we need it the most.

It is incredibly empowering to realize that no matter what happens from now on, our response to it will determine our results from it. If some frustrating surprise, setback, or circumstance lands in our lap in the future, we don't have to stay frustrated or wait for someone else to do something about it. We should always ask God for help, and then whatever *we* think, say, or do (or don't think, say, or do) about the situation will determine what we take away from it. This means that if we don't want negative results, we don't have to have them! We have the power to choose how to respond in a positive manner; our attitudes and actions will always determine what happens next.

Out of the Blue

I'll be honest, if I would have read something about rejection or abandonment while I was growing up, I probably would have *grasped* the concept, but I had virtually no point of reference about how it felt to be rejected or abandoned. I had the wonderful experience of growing up with both my mom and my dad in our home who expressed love and affection to me and my sisters on a regular basis. At school and church, I got along with most people and was surrounded by some great friends. I even got my fair share of attention from girls and had a few really nice girlfriends along the way.

But talk about surprises. I got the shock of my life and an introduction to rejection and abandonment all in one fell swoop in my late twenties when my twenty-something wife told me, "I love you. I'm just not *in love* with you anymore." Those were the most surprising and devastating words I had ever heard at that stage of my young life. My wife of nearly six years informed me that she thought we had gotten married too young and that she wasn't sure she wanted to continue our life together. Her aloof behavior leading up to her dropping that world-shaking bombshell on me suddenly started to make sense. She moved out of the house soon after that out-of-the-blue admission, which shook me to the core and initiated an extended period of sadness, numbness, and confusion.

Among a million other things, I questioned my own behavior—about what, if anything, I should have done differently. I wondered about whether or not my judgment had been off to have even married that girl in the first place. I seriously questioned my sense of self, my identity. In light of these developments, who exactly was I, anyway? And what in the world would I do with my future? When my head finally stopped rattling like a cartoon character who had just had his bell rung, but still feeling as though my guts had been ripped out and stomped on, I slowly realized that I alone had to determine how I would eventually, hopefully, emerge from the anguish. In the silence of a broken heart and shattered dream, I found plenty of time to mull over my options: Did I want to be a perpetual victim, always feeling sorry for myself, and hoping others would feel bad enough for me to help soothe my pain? Did I want to drown my sorrows? Could I escape? Could I numb the pain with noise? Should I just try to ignore it all to find some bliss? Or should I stop running from the hurting long enough to actually embrace and taste the pain? Could it be true that in the middle of such horrendous heartache, there might actually be healing? Was it possible that something good could emerge from my oh-so-dark days?

After transitioning out of one of the worst times in my life and having lived through other sad surprises since, I've started to ask fewer questions and accept that I won't always know why things happen the way they do. I am also now fully aware that my response to life circumstances determines my results.

If we do our best with what we're dealt, whether it's a bad hand or the luck of the draw, the odds of growing from it and eventually helping others through similar circumstances will be stacked in our favor. If we start to view our low points as future power spots, our tomorrows will be brighter!

8

BRAVE HEART

Have you ever had one of those experiences that caused you to reconsider what is really important in life? It may have been as simple as a heartfelt scene from a movie or as traumatic as the loss of someone you loved. More often than not, when something like that occurs, it sets in motion a shift in thinking that produces a different vantage point and things are never seen the same way.

After I was blindsided with my ex-wife's "not in love with you anymore" admission, I walked around dazed in a sad fog, feeling as if I'd had the wind knocked out of me. There were times I hurt so bad that as I laid my head on the pillow, I would entertain the thought of not waking up in the morning, which would be a welcome reprieve. But after a while, that nagging feeling of abandonment drove me to my knees. I started getting in the habit of kneeling in the shower each morning and often literally crying out to God, "I don't know what to do, but my eyes are on You." Though I didn't immediately become aware of what was happening, the view from my knees started elevating me and giving me a different perspective. Slowly, my mood improved, and I became increasingly aware of my altered outlook.

Years later, one of the guys I was coaching told me that he wanted to just walk away from his marriage. He said, "I just can't do it anymore." I empathized with his plight and talked with him about the rough spots that all relationships encounter. I said to him, "There's no doubt that marriage is not for the faint of heart." Yet at the same time I was disgusted with his decision to leave his wife. What kind of riled me up was his cavalier attitude about it. It reminded me of a line from a Keith Urban song: "These days it seems like everybody's just walking away, like there's no forever and love is just a game."[11]

But we know that love is not a game. It's not simple. Nor is it like an encounter with a cute little cupid, who throws red hearts and arrows and flowers and chocolates in our direction. It can be all-out war. Our Creator actually made us for connection, so it's no wonder that the field of love often feels like a battlefield. The one who comes to destroy us fights tooth and nail to cause disconnection in every relationship. So I got a little fired up over the idea of my friend just walking away from love because it had become inconvenient. I thought, *Really? What a coward.* No doubt my strong reaction stemmed from having somebody do that very same thing to me—just walk away. That had drastically influenced my view of love and highlighted the importance of expending every ounce of energy to keep my connections intact and healthy. I really wanted my friend to share my outlook, but, sadly, he didn't see it that way, and he eventually ended up just walking away from his wife.

The Heat of the Moment

Even just one instance of refused love can have a residual effect on us. Feelings of abandonment accumulate, and in our mind's eye, rejection is repetitive. It may have happened many years ago, but because our mind replays the hurtful memory so many times, it still feels like it happened yesterday. Those rejection reruns have a way of distorting reality, as we start to see everything through, not rose-colored glasses, but rejection-colored glasses. Psychologists say this sensitivity is common among people

---

11. John Shanks, Keith Urban, "My Heart Is Open," (Sony/ATV Music Publishing LLC), 2009.

who have been abandoned. They end up looking at life expecting to be rejected, left out, treated badly, or walked out on by friends or romantic partners.

FEELINGS OF ABANDONMENT ACCUMULATE, AND IN OUR MIND'S EYE, REJECTION IS REPETITIVE. IT MAY HAVE HAPPENED MANY YEARS AGO, BUT BECAUSE OUR MIND REPLAYS THE HURTFUL MEMORY SO MANY TIMES, IT STILL FEELS LIKE IT HAPPENED YESTERDAY.

For example, imagine spotting two coworkers walking down the hallway toward you. They are talking, but right after they make eye contact with you, one of them says something to the other, they both burst out laughing, and then they turn down another hallway, still laughing as they walk away. Now, if you have a rejection-colored view of the world, you will very likely assume that your coworkers were having a laugh at your expense and avoiding you. Keep in mind that if you were to approach them to ask about it, it's likely that their conversation had nothing to do with you. Maybe one of them was telling a funny story, or they were talking about a comedy they had seen, and you just happened to catch them in the middle of it. And all because they didn't immediately include you, you took it personally.

This kind of interpretation of situations becomes part of our everyday landscape if we have not yet responded properly to our history of hurts. Our view is tainted, and in our efforts to cope, we take out abandonment insurance and pay high premiums for rejection protection, whether or not we even realize it. Often this comes in the form of building walls around ourselves. We make strong resolutions for our future; nurse a quiet, inward determination, characterized by thoughts like, *Things will not always be this way*; and make emphatic declarations about our rights. Often we build these walls in the heat of the moment, when we think, say, or do things we don't really mean, like when the man I was coaching said, "I just can't do it anymore," even though he really loved his wife and wanted to be with her. His declaration had been in response to yet another blowout fight they had been having, so I'm sure it wasn't the first time he had vehemently declared something like that.

The thing is, when emotions are sky high and our rational thoughts are low, we say some things purely for shock value. We lash out either to shock other people or to please our base nature in that moment, because sometimes it just feels so good to say something bad! What we say may not even be that awful; it may be just some reaction to the moment. But our words have more power than we may ever realize, and we usually later regret what we have said, done, or left undone.

Very frequently our rash statements include the words *always* or *never*. We say things like, "That will never happen to me again!" "I'm always going to say whatever I want!" "I will never have kids!" "I will always spend money however I want to spend it!" "I will never let someone get that close to me again!" "That man hurt me—I will never trust men again!" "Ever since my boss betrayed me, I've always had a problem with authority!" "We never have any money!" "I guess we will always be broke!"

There are a couple of problems with these mental walls and verbal vows. First, the thief who wants to steal, kill, and destroy us is a meticulous note-taker. He has a record of pending charges against us; anything you say can and will be used against you. While it's true that bad stuff sometimes just happens; it's also true that other calamities occur because of the way we set our minds, mouths, or both, to invite them.

Second, when we do or say rash things, we are actually creating another layer of labels that can further smother our ability to connect to God, understand and love ourselves, and be open to loving others. We may think we are protecting ourselves, but we are actually sidelining ourselves. We are benching ourselves, isolating ourselves from others, and it is not healthy. When God made man, He said, *"It is not good for the man to be alone"* (Genesis 2:18).

When you're alone too long, you get weird. You start thinking that things are normal when they are absolutely anything but normal.

Remember the guy they called the "Unabomber"? Ted Kaczynski lived all by himself up in the mountains of Montana for years, when he started sending bombs through the mail to blow up innocent people, which is anything but normal. In seclusion, he had nobody to talk to about his ideas, and he actually got away with committing these heinous crimes for a while. Or consider hoarders. They typically live alone, and their obsession of collecting anything and everything isn't normal. And what about those with houses overrun with cats, whom are called "crazy cat" people? You get my point. We need people in our lives to ensure that we keep getting better, not worse.

True Colors

Research says that awareness and support are needed to break the perpetually hurtful cycles of rejection and abandonment. In other words, the rejection remedy is this: face the truth and learn to trust.

A problem we run into in the public arena, though, is that truth itself has taken such a beating that people have developed an aversion to it. Instead of "the whole truth and nothing but the truth," too many people opt for anything *but* the truth. While inside courtrooms, sworn oaths are supposed to make truth nonnegotiable, this is rarely the case outside the halls of justice. Fortunately, even though pure unadulterated truth is sometimes hard to find, it is easy to recognize. Authenticity and allegiance to truth are distinguishable qualities.

Disguising and running and hiding from the truth about what has hurt us only prolongs the problem and makes our circumstances more decayed by the day. If instead we bravely and vulnerably face the facts and deal with them as they are, even if knowledge of what to do next doesn't instantly materialize, we position ourselves to make better choices. The undeniably refreshing feeling that comes with having nothing to hide will become apparent in us. In being uncompromisingly honest, we are free to be ourselves, and with each breath of fresh air, we can breathe life into others, too.

Something to consider in this process is that all the hurtful, love-starved episodes we have endured are now part of our own unique experience. Our painful experiences have taught us many things, most importantly who we really are now. We've learned a lot about what we're made of, what we like and don't like, and what we absolutely will not tolerate. So those dilemmas that we would have loved to have avoided have actually shaped us, hopefully giving us a bravery that we never even knew was possible.

Another humongous truth to accept is that just because someone else, out of his or her own issues of insecurity, inferiority, jealousy, or just plain ignorance, has rejected or abandoned you does not mean that you are the one with the problem! Truly. Just because someone else took out his or her own frustrations on you does not mean you have to live with some sort of inferiority complex, or any other issue, for that matter. Embracing the truth that you were expertly designed to be connected to God and to others, and that you're not some type of damaged goods that deserves mistreatment, will allow you to view some good-byes as gifts instead of curses.

EMBRACING THE TRUTH THAT YOU WERE
EXPERTLY DESIGNED TO BE CONNECTED
TO GOD AND TO OTHERS, AND THAT YOU'RE
NOT SOME TYPE OF DAMAGED GOODS THAT
DESERVES MISTREATMENT, WILL ALLOW
YOU TO VIEW SOME GOOD-BYES AS GIFTS
INSTEAD OF CURSES.

Trust Fund

As I went through the emotional torture of an involuntary marriage separation, a constant stream of questioning ran through my mind. Along with the all-encompassing "why?" mind-set, I continued to mull over what I could have done differently, and I lived with the dull ache of wondering what was wrong with me. Eventually, as the months dragged on and the papers were filed and the divorce became final, my main train of thought was stuck on whether or not I'd ever be able to trust someone again.

After being hurt, it's natural to look back at the incident like a detective investigating a grisly crime scene. We rightfully delve into it, trying to uncover what part we played in the massacre of our feelings. We also wonder tirelessly about what we could have done to avoid it, all the while keeping a sharp lookout for ways to steer clear of a future brutality. But trying to protect ourselves by not trusting again is not nearly as safe as it sounds. In addition to divorce, I have experienced other relationship and business betrayals, followed by periods of time when I nursed the "once bitten twice shy" mentality. But I have come to understand that thinking that way keeps me in the "nothing ventured, nothing gained" category, too.

Unless someone plans to live in seclusion for the rest of his existence, trust is crucial for survival. Lowering defenses lets us see what is right in front of us and allows us to look further ahead at what is possible. Though we're on the battlefield of love, we have to lower our shield every now and then to see ahead and to move forward. That willingness to let down our guards in any relationship is a sign of good faith, and for me, the best place to start is with faith in God. Dipping into the trust fund of His limitless care helps me to be easier on myself and, in turn, withdraw the barriers, penalties, and restrictions I enforce to keep others out.

Sometimes people argue, "But if I trust again, I may get hurt again." It is true; this is a strong probability when other human beings are in the mix. But imagine a future of living the life of your dreams—all by yourself. It wouldn't be near as fulfilling as it could be if loved ones were there to experience it with you. Life's better when it's shared. I've found that the old adage "Better to have loved and lost than never to have loved at all"[12] can mean that lost love sets us up for *better love*. If I've found it to be true, so can you.

As I grow older, my focus has been to intentionally express love, and it's become increasingly clear that if a person is going to fight for any relationship that has passed the novelty or honeymoon phase, he must have a brave heart and a willingness to keep expressing love.

---

12. Alfred Tennyson, "In Memoriam A.H.H.," 1849.

After my heart had been shattered, I was convinced I would never care to be in a committed relationship again. But with the love of God; the support of family and close friends; along with the outlandishly wonderful experience of finding, falling in love with, and marrying the woman of my dreams, I'm glad to say I became fully convinced otherwise! I'm also not too modest to say that learning to trust and letting my walls down to allow access to a brutally wounded heart have continually required consistent bouts of bravery along the way. When I boldly went to God with my pain, He gave me a new view of my past, present, and future. My hurt and anger morphed into appreciation, and then turned into an anticipation of how things would work out for my future! And let me tell you, from experience, that things absolutely do get better!

Just about any changes in relationships, finances, or careers can cause plenty of soul-searching. Disruptions of the norm have a way of forcing our attention to the more valuable aspects of this beautiful life.

There will always be incidents that threaten love. When that happens, we would do well to take the Scripture's advice to guard our hearts. (See Proverbs 4:23.) But guarding our hearts does not always mean leaving the battle; it can mean being brave enough to stay in the battle, too. Running for the hills when the going gets tough means losing out on the spoils of war. And one of the biggest byproducts of peace with the past battle is resilience. Getting knocked down gives us the opportunity to get back up; and every time we get back up, we do it quicker and build up not only tolerance but confidence. Soon we'll start to think that if we can make it through *that*, we can make it through *anything*!

BUILDERS AND BLOCKERS:
REJECTION VERSUS AFFECTION

We were created for connection, so when the better-life blocker of *rejection* rears its ugly head, it plagues our core and corrupts so much of what we think, say, and do. Then, all too often, we end up repeating the same kind of behavior that originally hurt us, injuring others.

Rejection

To reject means to cast aside, throw away, shun, desert, give up, or forsake; and to refuse to give or receive love. To discover whether rejection is blocking your progress, take a look at this brief definition and the types of behavior it may cause us to display. Which of the following characteristics do you see in yourself?

How Rejection Looks and Acts

A person who rejects another is aloof; brushes off other people; gives them a cold shoulder; and dismisses, excludes, repels, scorns, and turns them down. They are often rebellious, refuses to answer for her actions, and has a hard time submitting to authority. This person is bitter at God and others, does not show proper respect for others, and finds it difficult to trust. They have a poor self-image, regular bouts of depression, and are prone to hopelessness. They often feel overly anxious and think that nobody cares. They are not comfortable in unfamiliar settings, extremely guarded and defensive, suspicious of new people, and have a tendency to isolate themselves. They can be terrified of intimacy or may smother anyone who gets close. They are extremely competitive, unbalanced, perfection-oriented (or totally disorganized), hypersensitive, easily upset, and overthink even the smallest of decisions.

Make It Personal

Resist the urge to think about someone else this may apply to. Be honest—this is about you. Take a moment to list any ways you see rejection evident in your present behavior.

Affection

Developing strong connections can't be done without the better-life builder of *affection*, a "fond attachment, devotion, or love…[an] emotion; feeling; [or] sentiment; the emotional realm of love."[13] To start getting a better understanding of affection, study this brief definition and the following description of how it looks and acts. Which of the following characteristics do you enjoy receiving? If you enjoy receiving them, perhaps you should consider developing them.

How Affection Looks and Acts

A person with affection for others is caring, charitable, friendly, generous, gracious, humble, kind, and tolerant. This person is accepting of and shows compassion to people of all backgrounds. They are courteous, hospitable, and make every effort to make others comfortable. They are also gracious, tactful, service-oriented, and always willing to put others

---

13. "affection," *Dictionary.com*, http://www.dictionary.com/browse/affection?s=t.

before themselves. They display a patient, gentle demeanor; are not rude, easily angered, or offended; and are always loyal. They are never arrogant, boastful, or jealous. They refuse to talk negatively about others, and they celebrates others' successes.

Affection Building Material

Repetition builds skill. So take time daily to build your better life by thinking, praying, and/or saying:

> Jesus replied, "You must love the LORD your God with all your heart, all your soul, and all your mind." This is the first and greatest commandment. A second is equally important: "Love your neighbor as yourself." The entire law and all the demands of the prophets are based on these two commandments.   (Matthew 22:37–40)

> Love is patient and kind. Love is not jealous or boastful or proud or rude. It does not demand its own way. It is not irritable, and it keeps no record of being wronged. It does not rejoice about injustice but rejoices whenever the truth wins out. Love never gives up, never loses faith, is always hopeful, and endures through every circumstance.
>   (1 Corinthians 13:4–7)

Make It Personal

Before moving on, take some time to practice the "3-R's." Ask yourself the following questions and apply them to your life.

Reflect

1. What did I relate to the most in what I just read?

2. Who are my closest connections?

3. Do I have to earn affection in any of these relationships? If so, how?

4. Do I feel like I'm damaged goods? Why?

5. Have I hurt others in the same way I have been hurt? Whom? How?

6. The main languages of love and affection are time, touch, words, gifts, and service. How do I best show my love?

Release

If there is anything you need to let go of, repeat the following: "After reflecting, I see that I need to let go of _____, and I choose to release it now." Then pray this Scripture:

Search me, God, and know my heart; test me and know my anxious thoughts. See if there is any offensive way in me, and lead me in the way everlasting. (Psalm 139:23–24 NIV)

Renew

After consciously letting go of what's been weighing on you, what are some positive things you can commit to in the future?

Dear friends, let us love one another, for love comes from God. Everyone who loves has been born of God and knows God. Whoever does not love does not know God, because God is love. (1 John 4:7–8 NIV)

 PART 5

PEACE WITH THE PAST:
WHEN CAN I FINALLY
STOP HURTING?

9

▄▖ THAT WAS THEN

Upon his wife's proposals for new furniture, paint, and updated décor of their home, a man asked, "Why change everything now? There's no need for it," sounding very much set in his ways. "I want things to stay just the way they are."

He sounds like a lot of us—not especially interested in change. Even when change knocks on our door with a promise of something better, we do our best to ignore its loud, incessant pounding.

It won't go away, though. Everything changes. Times change. People change. Neighborhoods, churches, jobs, and governments change. And if we're smart, we'll "turn and face the strange," as David Bowie sang in his classic song, "Changes."[14]

It has been said that to continue to do the same thing and expect a different result is insanity. But if we want to make peace with our past, we would be wise to follow what Romans 12:2 says and *be transformed by the renewing of your mind*" (NIV). If we don't stay open to new things in an ever-evolving world of fashion and technology, we run the risk of becoming

---

14. David Bowie, "Changes," (Peermusic Publishing, Sony/ATV Music Publishing LLC, Warner/Chappell Music, Inc.), 1971.

outdated. Although it may not be absolutely necessary to have the latest cell phone—or in the case of the change-challenged husband, the latest furniture and decorations—we should know that a brighter tomorrow requires that we learn new ways of doing things today. As time ticks by, our willingness to change will keep us current or even ahead of time.

Time Change

One morning I bought a newspaper, only to realize that it was yesterday's paper! Nobody wants yesterday's news. But too many times, we allow yesterday's stories to pile up on us. We get angry that our boss didn't go to bat for us, or stressed out about a call we received from the doctor's office. Mounting debt, blended families, or the betrayal by a friend can weigh us down. Then we overanalyze the circumstances until we work ourselves into a frenzy, making our body ache or making us so tense that we can't sleep. Being on edge causes us to snap at people, creating even more situations to juggle. How do we usually handle it? We worry more and repeat the same cycle. Carrying the weight of yesterday's news can make us feel something like impending doom today.

Most likely, since you picked up this book in the first place, times have not been turning out quite like you had planned. Problems in our work, health, finances, relationships, and really, just about any area of life, can make it seem like we are light-years away from fulfilling our dreams. But does that mean we should just give up on dreams coming true? I hope not. No matter what has or hasn't happened in the past, things in the present are still moving, still changing. Now may be the perfect time to embrace the new and finally adjust our mind-sets to start handling some things differently.

Making peace with the past requires that we stay active in designing our lives in the present and in the ultimate future. Letting the past run our lives would be like letting a caboose run a train. It doesn't look right, it's not natural, and it won't get us very far—that's for sure. Hopefully, by this point, no matter where you are in your journey, you are starting to understand that there will always be a battle between the past and the present that will impact the future. It is a lifelong battle requiring necessary adjustments just to keep pace and move forward.

MAKING PEACE WITH THE PAST REQUIRES THAT WE STAY ACTIVE IN DESIGNING OUR LIVES IN THE PRESENT AND IN THE ULTIMATE FUTURE.

If we've been seriously hurt, whether in childhood, adolescence, or any stage of life, we probably have defense mechanisms and protection patterns, and perhaps warped perceptions and out-of-control emotions, which are hard habits to break. But because it requires a "3-peat" of practice, patience, and perseverance to get better, sadly, some people just hug the security blanket of the familiar and shun change. Fearing change is in itself a bad habit. Benjamin Franklin summed up the absolute necessity of forward motion when he said, "When you're finished changing, you're finished."

Maybe you want to stay angry, bitter, self-destructive, unforgiving, depressed, and generally out of control. It could be that you actually enjoy being the victim, having a big chip on your shoulder and blaming everybody but yourself for your troubles. Then again, I doubt it. You're likely not the "Debbie Downer" type of person, or you wouldn't have made it this far into this book. But if you have been that kind of person, all that is about to change. How do I know? Because throughout these pages, you probably have had a few moments of truth about your background and identity, which have prepared you to finally leave some things behind.

Mad About You

To recover what we've lost and discover what can be ours, we must understand some of the biggest contributors to bad behavior patterns—bitterness, resentment, and unforgiveness. The root cause of these toxic triplets is most often disappointment or anger over an injustice we have suffered.

When we're feeling stung by a violation of our rights, it's perfectly normal and healthy to be angry. Anger is a natural human feeling. This adrenaline-inducing emotion is part of God's design to keep us safe. However, anger, by definition, is a "strong, usually temporary, displeasure without specifying manner of expression."[15] We know for sure that anger is strong. No doubt about it. We've all witnessed the way displeasure, in ours and others' lives, can produce powerful, Hulk-like reactions. But it's the "usually temporary" part of anger's definition that is easy to overlook. "Usually temporary" means that anger is to be a fleeting emotion, not a way of life. Our anger is much like a carton of milk, which has an expiration date. We all know what happens when milk passes its expiration date—it spoils and it stinks! So what happens when we hold on to anger or any other emotion too long? If we don't learn healthy ways to express it, and move on, it could turn toxic!

Manners of expressing anger differ from person to person. Expressions vary from silent, undetectable sadness or depression, to visible pouts and chip-on-the-shoulder attitudes, to unmistakable outbursts of blind rage that we see all too often in the news. People don't always stick with just one expression, either. Many display anger in different ways, but most have their favorites.

Some like to romanticize it, treating their animosity or depression like a love interest, mulling over it again and again, keeping it in the forefront of their minds at all times. For others, anger is fuel for dreaming up worst-case scenarios to wish on their offenders. Others wear anger on their sleeves, just waiting for someone to cross them in the slightest manner so they can fly off the handle. Still others let anger define what they will and will not do. They may say things like, "I can't spend any more time with this person, because of what she did"; "I'll never go to that place again, because of what happened"; and "I absolutely won't ever do that again, because of what occurred."

Hot or Not

You may or may not have known why so many people, including yourself, behave badly every day, but now that you're getting familiar with it, hopefully you'll know it when you see it.

---

15. *The American Heritage Dictionary.*

It could have been the heat, but one day a few summers back, I had a few encounters with people who were irritable, mean, or just downright rude. From the waitress with a bad attitude to the suit salesmen who seemed mad at the world, it became amazingly apparent that anger was not a good look for anyone in the summer or in any other season.

After a string of those situations, I started to notice that others' bad moods and attitudes can easily slip off of them and onto me. When that happens, it causes me to feel draped with anger and frustration. I'm embarrassed to say that my wife witnessed me wearing ugly attitudes and actions too many times that year. I really didn't want to be that way; I can't stand being treated rudely, and the last thing I'd want to do is treat others that way, especially those closest to me. Wearing ugly feelings on our sleeves is destructive, not to mention completely counterproductive. It doesn't look good on anybody, and it dismantles things we've worked hard to establish, projects we've put a lot of time and effort into, and our biggest accomplishments of all—our relationships.

WEARING UGLY FEELINGS ON OUR SLEEVES IS DESTRUCTIVE, NOT TO MENTION COMPLETELY COUNTERPRODUCTIVE.

Every day, there are opportunities for us to pick up and put on somebody's anger. I had it happen to me one afternoon as I was working out. When I finished my final set of shoulder exercises on a machine, a guy stepped up and asked, "How many more sets do you have to do?"

Ready to move on to the free weights, I told him that I had finished, and bent over to pick up my water bottle off the floor. When I straightened up, he had moved closer to me, standing with a defiant look on his face, and muttered, "You took long enough."

Hearing the antagonistic tone of his voice, I instantly felt a hot flush of anger rise in me and thought, *Uh-oh*. But instead of reacting in a combative manner, I looked him in the eyes, smiled real big, and said, "Well, you'll just have to get here before me next time." Then I walked away.

On the other side of the gym, I still felt an adrenaline rush from that potentially unpleasant situation I had just avoided, but as I picked up a barbell to continue my workout, I also felt relieved and somewhat proud of myself. I silently celebrated my progress by thanking to God for the strength to be pleasant and walk away. I grinned as I hoisted the weight from my waist to my chin, and actually recalled a few admonitions about the dangers of being hot-tempered:

> *People with understanding control their anger; a hot temper shows great foolishness.* (Proverbs 14:29)

> *A fool is quick-tempered, but a wise person stays calm when insulted.* (Proverbs 12:16)

> *A hot-tempered person starts fights; a cool-tempered person stops them.* (Proverbs 15:18)

Keeping cool, being pleasant, and walking away has not always been my response to those touchy types of situations. Overheating was more like it. So I was grateful when I recognized that my consistent efforts to [B]etter had paid off. I'm nowhere near perfection, that's for sure, but I have made advancements in my behavior. God only knows what would have happened if I had given that man my old staple response—a sarcastic comment and a disgusted look. It's pretty accurate to imagine that my workout probably would have included some boxing that day, resulting in a beat-up life rather than a better life.

Sandpaper

I bet you've had incidents like that happen to you, too. Or maybe there are some people in your life who have a tendency to get under your skin. You know the ones. They always seem to know exactly how to push your buttons. I imagine one of the disciples fell into that very category leading up to Jesus' death. Luke 22:3 (NIV) says, *"Then Satan entered Judas, called Iscariot, one of the Twelve."*

Isn't that crazy? I mean, think about it, if Satan could infiltrate someone who had been physically walking and talking with Jesus, witnessing His lifestyle and miracles firsthand, how much more do we need to be on guard against his subtle influence? Every day, Satan issues endless invitations and orchestrates all types of situations to get us to give in to our lower nature. When he attempts to get into our heads with painful reminders of our past—or with thoughts like, *Don't back down; You don't have to take that; Fight for your rights*—and we don't give in, more than likely he will try to mess with us another way, or will slither away to infiltrate someone else's mind.

Judas proves that the old saying "There's one in every bunch" really is true. There are times when we all have to deal with difficult people. Periodically, bosses, coworkers, family members, and even friends can ruffle our feathers—not to mention the casual acquaintances and people we interact with on a daily basis who clearly have never learned the meaning of common courtesy.

Every time the sun comes up, there will be plenty of chances for us to get mad and madder, and stay mad. It seems like many people show more anger every day, even though most of us have heard it said that we should not go to bed angry, which is a potentially lifesaving piece of advice that actually comes from the Bible: *"'Don't sin by letting anger control you.' Don't let the sun go down while you are still angry, for anger gives a foothold to the devil"* (Ephesians 4:26–27). When we let anger control us, we get played like a puppet and usually end up looking foolish.

Fight and Flight

There's no doubt I've played the fool many times. I was a huge fool one particular time when I was trying to make my way through the overly crowded LAX airport to catch a flight. While navigating the anger-inducing exercise in patience known as the security checkpoint, my wife and I heard my name repeatedly announced over the loudspeaker: "Randal Smalls, please report to Gate 22."

After finally making it through security, I hurried to the gate, where an agent greeted me with a major dose of attitude! He appeared to take pleasure in informing me that he had given away our first-class upgrade and had separated our seats on the flight because we had not checked in at the gate earlier. Having already been building frustration throughout the excruciatingly long security line, I felt fully justified in matching the agent's lousy attitude and demanded that he give us our reserved exit row seats back! His sarcastic reaction made my blood boil, resulting in a full-on angry shouting match! I wrote down his name, the flight number, gate number, and a few notes to share with his superiors as soon as I had the chance, but he remained defiant. Needless to say, I didn't succeed in convincing him to return our seats, and I was still hot under the collar and madder than a wet hen!

Later, as the plane reached its cruising altitude, I still felt that my anger had been justified, and still planned to file a complaint about how I had flown over a million miles with them and didn't deserve to be treated that way—blah, blah, blah, blah…. But then I was reminded of my model for anger in Psalm 30:5: "[God's] *anger lasts only a moment, but his favor lasts a lifetime!*"

There I was, "The Better Life Coach," flying across the US to conduct a private better-life event, having just acted like a complete idiot in front of strangers—and, even worse, in front of my wife. I had played the fool, alright. It hit me, as it had many times before, how eternally grateful I was that God doesn't stay mad at me. And if He doesn't stay mad, I'm not allowed to stay mad, either. I was suddenly aware that the expiration date on my anger was fast approaching. Right then and there, at thirty thousand feet in the air, I asked for God's forgiveness and let the issue go. By swallowing my pride, I let the anger run its course and become a fleeting emotion instead of a way of life.

Why do we allow ourselves to get so heated over the littlest things, anyway? I mean, honestly, is it really necessary that I get completely incensed when a person in the car in front of me decides to stop at a yellow light, forcing me to slam on my brakes? Is it worth it to feel enraged when a person in the express checkout line has more than twelve items? Oh, and I wonder if, to keep from becoming unglued, I really need to find out whoever it was who didn't clean up his mess in the break-room microwave.

Is it okay to think and feel that way on a regular basis? Generally, when stuff like that happens, aside from my run-in with the guy at the airport, we don't usually confront the ones who have inconvenienced us. They never see us engulfed in the heat of displeasure or slink away to a corner to silently brood with a pint of ice cream and a spoon. In most cases, our frustration manifests only inside of us, and the symptoms show up in our bodies—our faces are flushed, our ears are hot, or our waistlines expand as we eat to find comfort. We let our minds race with unpleasant thoughts directed toward those who violated us—those clueless ones who haven't realized that the world revolves around us. I guess it doesn't matter if you want to think and feel that way—unless you're committed to living better.

Even though most of us know that we're not supposed to let the sun go down on our anger, we haven't been aware of the Scripture's invitation to live at a level of life in which anger is but a fleeting emotion. A calm, peaceful demeanor that isn't easily rattled by much of anything can be more than just a behavior we admire in others—it can be ours! Living in our fast-paced, short-fused world, it has become increasingly obvious to me that my own resolve to make my love known to God, myself, and others will require me to be slow to anger and to keep no record of wrongs.

A CALM, PEACEFUL DEMEANOR THAT ISN'T EASILY RATTLED BY MUCH OF ANYTHING CAN BE MORE THAN JUST A BEHAVIOR WE ADMIRE IN OTHERS—IT CAN BE OURS!

Instead of allowing the issues of the past to pile up and bog us down, maybe we could take a lesson from that daily newspaper I mentioned earlier. Think about it, every day a new issue of the newspaper comes out with story lines that are relevant to that day. Sure, there are some ongoing stories that make the headlines, but there are always new developments to report, as well. At the end of the day, what will you do? Will you hold on to that paper, allowing yesterday's news to bog you down, or will you recycle or throw away that newspaper, making room for the new one and the new stories that will arrive tomorrow?

How can I possibly throw away the old stories? Well, you have to decide that the time is right to take on a different view of all those stories of past blowups, beatdowns, and instances of being rubbed the wrong way. Since we deal with difficult people so often, there's a pretty good chance that those bumps in the road are part of a bigger story to help us improve. I mean, consider Judas' bad behavior—it actually turned out to be a part of the bigger picture of humanity's redemption.

Some of the most famously successful people took a different look at adversity. Walt Disney was fired by a newspaper editor for lack of creativity. Michael Jordan was demoted from his high-school varsity team to junior varsity, deemed "too short" for varsity basketball. The Beatles were rejected by a record company executive who told them, "Guitar groups are on their way out." So maybe all these incidents and accidents, and the pain-in-the-neck people and their opinions of us—whether way back when or earlier today—have done us a favor. If we look at it that way, we may start to see how their actions can work like sandpaper, smoothing out our rough edges. And without rough edges, we won't create as much friction in the moves we make, allowing for smoother transitions from one level of better life to another.

10

▛ HERE AND NOW

I read an article about a nineteen-year-old from Nebraska named Robert who walked into an Omaha mall around Christmastime in 2007 and fired an AK-47 machine gun, killing eight people and then himself. An investigative reporter wrote that just before the murderous rampage, Robert had lost his job and broken up with his girlfriend. Throughout his childhood and adolescence, he'd experienced several traumatic events along with other common issues, but he had never expressed his pain, anger, or struggles to anyone. Time after time, he'd just hidden his feelings by stuffing them down inside himself. Robert's sad story confirms the truth in Jesus' statement in Matthew 10:26 (NIV): "*There is nothing concealed that will not be disclosed, or hidden that will not be made known.*"

When we hide our offenses, hurts, habits, and demons we're fighting—or, like another mass shooter in Alabama did, keep a list of who harmed us and what went wrong—we build up an immense amount of torment in our brains and in our bodies. And when pressure builds up like that, it will eventually find its way back outside, usually at times, in places, and in ways we least expect it. Sometimes things seep out; other times they explode.

Take your hall closet, for example. If you continually stuff things in there and quickly shut the door (as we've done too often at my house), eventually it will become so full that it can't contain any more. All those coats, boots, Christmas decorations, board games, and golf clubs will come spilling out, making a mess that's hard to hide. This same type of thing has gone on year after year in some of our lives. We have bottled up injustices for so long that now every time we get a little shaken up, we blow up. Issues may have surfaced in the forms of stress, hypersensitivity, violence, nagging sadness, fits of rage, lack of energy, health problems, thoughts of suicide, or other seemingly random, out-of-character behaviors.

Those of us who want to do more than just cope with unpleasantries have to learn healthy ways of releasing what is pressing on us. Pressure relief can be as simple as going for a walk; working out at the gym; playing a favorite sport; or getting out the hose, a bucket, and some soap to wash our cars. There are probably as many different activities of release as there are people on the planet, because everybody is different. But for my money, expressing thoughts, issues, questions, or concerns in writing is particularly therapeutic. Keeping a journal allows me to formulate the contents of my mind into some sort of structure, which can then be used in the most effective manner of relief: talking to God and/or people I trust.

Expressing our concerns to God in an open and honest fashion, and then taking time to listen to an understanding, compassionate, and merciful God, has a miraculous way of prompting health and healing from the inside out. And when we need human interaction, there's no substitute for a confidential conversation with a wise mentor, coach, close friend, or loved one. When you have pressing issues, don't run the risk of ignoring them and letting them linger.

EXPRESSING OUR CONCERNS TO GOD IN AN OPEN AND HONEST FASHION, AND THEN TAKING TIME TO LISTEN TO AN UNDERSTANDING, COMPASSIONATE, AND MERCIFUL GOD, HAS A MIRACULOUS WAY OF PROMPTING HEALTH AND HEALING FROM THE INSIDE OUT.

Time to Burn

When time and anger intertwine, things heat up. The longer an offense goes unresolved, the more deeply it is rooted in a person. If we are not swift in responding to burning issues, then our hearts become hotbeds for bitterness, resentment, and unforgiveness, which, as the Latin origin of the word *anger* suggests, slowly strangle us. When conflicts arise, our natural response is to rise up and protect what is ours, also known as the fight-or-flight response. What is unnatural is when we brood over some wrong for extended periods of time. If we don't stamp it out quickly, we can't protect what's ours—we just create a fast-moving fire that chars everything in its path. In much the same way as the number of lives saved in an emergency sometimes depends on how fast first responders can respond to it, the sooner we respond to our own fires, the greater the chances of our survival and success.

As I mentioned, most of us developed our expressions of anger very early, likely as small children. The patterns are generally established through positive or negative reinforcement, or rewarded or punished behavior. We learned how to get attention or, as in the Omaha mall shooter's case, to go unnoticed. By now, we have acted this way for so long that it has become a habit. One all-too-common habit people have developed is going to bed angry, believing that it's okay because they're not really mad at other people, just angry with themselves.

However, according to health professionals, internalizing anger can be a potentially life-threatening problem. Some health professionals and educators have said that buried anger may soon outrank the risks of smoking and obesity, leading to chronic diseases and premature death. Some have argued that bitterness and resentment actually prevent the liver and gallbladder from getting rid of toxins, which puts people at a higher probability for developing, among other things, ulcers and arthritis, as well as having heart attacks and strokes. Their research confirms a recurring theme in Proverbs—that *"runaway emotions corrode the bones"* (Proverbs 14:30 MSG). Yes, getting angry is natural, but staying angry could be terminal. Remember what I said in chapter 9, "That Was Then"? When we hold on to hard feelings past their expiration date, they spoil and decay and can make us sick. Buried anger ferments into poison, and it doesn't remain in just one area—it spreads. It is just like getting bit by a snake—the longer the venom stays in the body, the more far-reaching its effects.

Outbreak

When a friend of mine told me that he had been fired from the family-owned company he worked at for years, I was sympathetic. When he went on to tell me that his brother-in-law had fired him, I was indignant. I mean, can you imagine the anger and frustration you would feel going through something that horrible? I didn't blame him for having had awful thoughts about the guy, or for refusing to talk to him or his wife.

While the situation was still smoldering, his family members had taken sides in the squabble. Heated exchanges had taken place, and a lot of nasty things had been said, while some siblings had just completely stopped talking. Their family business environment had suffered, family functions had been tense, and some regular get-togethers had been scrapped altogether to avoid further altercations. As my friend held on to his hurt, his bitterness indeed became a poisonous resentment, complete with a dead-set determination to not forgive the ones involved until hell had sufficiently frozen over.

Nearly five years of diminishing family relationships, mental turmoil, and curious physical pains had passed by the time I was introduced to this man who became my friend. It was not long after he became involved in "The Better Life Course," which really helped him grasp why he had experienced so much turmoil, that he discovered the source of all that had been ailing him in Ephesians 4:31–32 (NIV):

> *Get rid of all bitterness, rage and anger, brawling and slander, along with every form of malice. Be kind and compassionate to one another, forgiving each other, just as in Christ God forgave you.*

So he decided that enough was enough. He swallowed his pride and went to meet with his brother-in-law. He told him that he was ready to let go of the firing incident, and he asked for forgiveness for holding a stubborn grudge for so long.

The bitterness and resentment that had raged out of control in his heart all those years were then dismissed with his brother-in-law's nonchalant response: "Yeah, sure." Not exactly the climactic reconciliation one might hope for, but it was one nonetheless, that kick-started the process of containing the outbreak and allowing the healing to begin.

Fallout

Every relationship goes through seasons of highs and lows. There are warm times when we feel extra close to a friend, spouse, coworker, or family member; and then there are cold spells when we feel millions of miles apart. There are also times when damage is so drastic and so deep that people are boiling mad enough to consider burning bridges with others. A rift develops due to a sharp disagreement or a case of betrayal, as in my friend's case. It's not out of the ordinary to hear of people who go their separate ways and eliminate all contact. "We had a falling out" is usually what we hear to describe those incidents. It's sad when that happens, because unless one of the parties takes the initiative to repair that relationship, it will be forever lost, leaving a void the size of a person.

Strife is nothing new, of course. The Bible tells how the apostle Paul and his buddy Barnabas had a falling out that lasted several years. At some point, perhaps they remembered one of King Solomon's proverbs, which labeled quarrelers as fools (see Proverbs 20:3), or Jesus' teaching on how peacemakers were sons of God (see Matthew 5:9). There's even a good chance Paul had Barnabas in the back of his mind when he wrote about unity and maturity in the body of Christ in Ephesians 4. Whatever brought them back together, they did eventually come to their senses, repair their relationship, and become great friends again.

I believe that except in cases of abusive situations, burning bridges ought to be considered against our religion. Relationships produce opportunities; burning bridges torches them. Rebuilding bridges builds a better life. Quick resolutions can salvage things before they completely go up in flames. Disagreements happen. Misunderstandings happen. People have bad days and say things they don't mean. People might even get mad for no apparent reason and may take it out on us. But that doesn't mean it's time to put that partnership out to pasture for good. It may just mean that some time apart is needed.

RELATIONSHIPS PRODUCE OPPORTUNITIES; BURNING BRIDGES TORCHES THEM. REBUILDING BRIDGES BUILDS A BETTER LIFE.

Many times, we can deal with our burning issues more quickly than we do. Maturity requires taking the initiative to keep relationships from falling out or to help put them back in place. Maybe the next time a fight breaks out, walk to the other side of the house, or to the other side of town, depending on how much the feud has escalated. Count to ten, or ten thousand, whatever it takes. Just don't say or do anything drastic. Let off some steam and think it over. Then re-approach the situation with the added perspective, resolved to act as a peacemaker, not a fool.

Beyond Reason

At one time or another, I believe most of us have had, or still do have, what I call "reasonable resentments"—resentments that are justifiable. Someone did something horribly wrong to you, or some horrible situation happened to you, and upon hearing your full story, nobody in his right mind would disagree that you have just cause to be angry. Perhaps one or several of those instances are still smoldering or raging inside of you, hurting you and keeping you from making peace with the past. But if you've decided to journey into a better life, ask yourself this question: does the wrong make it right for me to keep carrying it around and quite possibly pass it on to others?

You may say, "It is my life—I have the right to be angry." I guess you have the right to carry around toxic emotions, slowly poisoning your own spirit, mind, and body; you will hurt only yourself, for a little while, anyway. But because poison spreads, no matter how hard you try to contain it, eventually it will seep into other areas and affect more than just you. You're going to poison other people. Most likely, it will start to affect the people closest to you, and they will continue to get the biggest doses of it. And that's *not* right; in fact, it's selfish, unfair, and *un*reasonable.

For all the God-fearing folks, think of it this way: Does God have *just cause* to forgive and forget our faults? Do we need to justify why God should remove our sins and screw-ups *"as far from us as the east is from the west"* (Psalm 103:12)? Or does He just simply do it because we ask Him?

Think of something awful you've done, something for which you've already received forgiveness. Did you have to give God at least one good reason why He should forgive you? No. You didn't, I didn't, nobody has ever had to do that, nor will anyone *ever* have to do that. God knows He can hold our sins against us; but He still forgives us, anyway. He completely releases us from all our debts.

You could say that God is unreasonable that way. Our finite minds can't comprehend how He's able to do that. We just don't get it. Good thing we don't have to—we just get to accept it. The only responsibility we have to make that deal valid is to forgive our debtors. Jesus taught us to pray, *"Forgive us our debts, **as** we forgive our debtors"* (Matthew 6:12 KJV, emphasis added). If we don't forgive others, we are the ones who shrink our world into a prison. But if we release others, even without a good reason, we'll discover that we have really freed ourselves.

Open Air

Sometimes, when I crave the freedom of open spaces, I open all the windows and the sunroof in my truck. Enjoying that fresh air rushing in as I drive down the road often reminds me of summertime as a kid. My sister, cousins, and I loved to ride in the open air of my Uncle Jim's truck bed, yelling, smiling, and laughing with the wind blowing in our faces.

As we grow older, some of us lose that free-and-happy feeling. We become more bottled up and closed off. Instead of having our "windows down," so to speak, we feel as if they have been barred or boarded up altogether. Various things can cause it, but one of the biggest reasons our creativity and contentment feel stifled is a lack of forgiveness for all those burning issues.

Why all the talk of forgiveness? Why do we even want to be forgiven or give forgiveness, anyway? What is the benefit? Scripture puts it in pretty simple terms: *"In this man Jesus there is forgiveness for your sins! Everyone who trusts in him is freed from all guilt and declared righteous"* (Acts 13:38–39 TLB). So basically, along with the assurance of being right with God, forgiveness of sins gives us freedom from guilt. Guilt is such a restrictive feeling. It keeps us from being ourselves, weighs heavily on us, and suffocates so much of what we do. But when we ask Jesus for forgiveness, He miraculously lifts the weight from our shoulders and frees our minds.

Asking God or someone else for forgiveness, whether for something we did ten minutes ago or ten years ago, whether for the first time or the hundred and first time, is like opening the windows of our soul. It lets out the stuffy and suffocating feelings of guilt, condemnation, bitterness, and resentment, and lets fresh air in, so we can breathe easier and live better. To make peace with our past, some of us need to forgive ourselves, but every one of us needs forgiveness from God and, most likely, from others, and for others.

Asking for forgiveness from others? Yes. For a better life, there's no way around it. And that's a good thing. When my friend made the choice to forgive his brother-in-law, who experienced the freedom? It didn't sound like his brother-in-law did, did it? No, my friend experienced the freedom. Oh, and remember my run-in with the airport agent I told you about in the last chapter? The story didn't end with my plea for forgiveness thirty-thousand feet in the air. I also said to God, "If I ever see that guy again, I'll ask him for forgiveness, too."

Well, I had completely forgotten about that part of the prayer. That is, until two weeks later, as I was winding my way through the same security checkpoint to catch a flight at the same gate! Suddenly, I was reminded of my prayer in the air: *If I ever see that guy again, I'll ask him for forgiveness, too.* Oh, man—how I hoped that guy wasn't there that day! But as I slowly slinked toward the gate, peeking around the corner, my fingers crossed, guess who I saw standing at the check-in podium? That's right—that guy!

I swallowed hard and walked right up to him. I introduced myself and reminded him who I was and how we hadn't gotten along so well the last time I was there. When a look of recognition mixed with a bit of annoyance came across his face, I told him I was sorry for acting like a jerk. I asked him to forgive me, and offered my hand, saying that I hoped we could be friends. He smiled, shook my hand, and told me he was sorry, too, explaining that he'd had a super crazy day and had flown off the handle. I said, "Hey, we all have those days, don't we?"

Then I walked away to get in line to board the plane. About a minute later, he walked over to me and told me that I was the second person in his twenty-six years with the airline that had ever apologized after such an incident, of which there had been way too many to count. He thanked me, apologized again for his behavior, and said, "Yes, I think we can be friends."

That was several years ago, and to this day, almost every time I go through that airport terminal, I see my friend Kevin, the supervising gate agent. He still gets a kick out of having gotten into a shouting match with "The Better Life Coach," and we laugh about it and swap stories about the other people we've told about our Gate-22 blowup. Most times, when he sees me, he goes to his computer and starts typing away, seeing if he can work his magic to get me a better seat on my flight. I sure am thankful that forgiveness was a part of this story; if I had just let that bridge burn, then every time I saw him, he may have gone to his computer and reassigned me to the worst seat on the plane! Yes, forgiveness is a very good thing.

Storytellers

Throughout this book, you have read a lot of stories about the ups and downs of building a better life; some are my own, and others I've collected firsthand. I started appreciating the value of a good story way back when I was a little boy. As my mom would wash my hair every Saturday night so I'd be clean for church Sunday morning, my regular request was "Mom, could you tell me a story?" One of my all-time favorite stories was of my great-grandfather who killed a huge black snake with only a rake while working out in the field. Afterward, people came from miles around to witness his amazing conquest.

Scripture tells us, *"We can comfort those in any trouble with the comfort we ourselves receive from God"* (2 Corinthians 1:4 NIV). I don't know if I was comforted by the actual stories back then or not. It may have been that I just found comfort in the storyteller, my mom. One thing I do know, though, is that God's comfort has been present in all the trouble I've faced in improving the quality of my life and helping others do the same. The comforting qualities and life lessons drawn from Jesus' earthly experiences and timeless parables are collectively known as "The Greatest Story Ever Told." No matter what we face, we can always draw strength from His life story to include in the chronicles we are writing simply by living every day.

I hope you've been strengthened as you read these stories, too, and that it will help you write a better story—because you've got one, too. There is something extremely therapeutic about sharing your own life and stories with someone. Interestingly enough, the therapy of self-disclosure works both ways. Every time we tell a story, lessons from that experience become clearer in our own minds, while the reader or listener is able to identify with what we've said, and may realize that they are not alone in their feelings and struggles.

THERE IS SOMETHING EXTREMELY THERAPEUTIC ABOUT SHARING YOUR OWN LIFE AND STORIES WITH SOMEONE.

I remember being approached by a young man after a better-life group session with inner-city teenagers. I had told of my struggle as a teenager to end a relationship with a girl because our lives were headed in opposite directions. At that time, I had known for a while that I needed to end it but procrastinated because I was too cozy in the relationship and didn't want to be alone. The young man told me that he was in almost the exact same situation, wrestling with whether or not he could actually let go of the girl, but now he clearly knew what he had to do and felt strong enough to do it.

Willingness to tell on yourself, especially your less-than-perfect qualities and experiences, does not make you look weak. Self-disclosure displays self-confidence and strengthens your positive influence and authenticity in the eyes of others.

Back in the Game

One of the first times I accompanied a friend to a 12-step meeting—an event built around self-disclosure—at the end of the night, the regular attendants of the group bid us and everyone else good-bye with "Keep coming back. It works." I remember thinking it was a nice, subtle way to remind people about the ongoing nature of battling an addiction. I thought about how the climb toward control in the fight with a potentially debilitating disease requires consistent effort. In the same way we pursue a better life by continually fighting the demons of addiction, we must leave our past behind so we can advance to new levels.

Often, the demons with the loudest voices are the ones that, with concerted effort, try to pull our attention back toward our hurts and tainted history. They regularly run the lowlight reel of our past failures and far-from-saintly actions, simultaneously pointing out our glaring lack of qualifications to ever be anything more than what we've always been.

If you and I are going to experience life beyond what has been, we have to "keep coming back" to love. We have to be tenacious in our efforts to keep no record of wrongs. People who make progress forgive themselves and others, and keep coming back to give their best, no matter how badly they have blown it.

I've noticed that, in the rush toward our goals, we drop the ball from time to time. You know what? So what! Don't hang your head and run to the sideline. You're not disqualified. Pick it back up and keep running. If I make a mistake and fall flat on my face, what should I do? Should I stay down, go into isolation, and keep beating myself up over being a repeat offender of the same wrong? Whose cause would I help by doing that? At my age, I've done enough stupid things in my lifetime to know that if I act that way, I certainly won't help my cause, or anybody else's, for that matter.

After a tumble, I've found the quickest way to get back on the right track is to look up to God, confess my sin, and plead for His mercy and forgiveness. Receiving His mercy allows me to forgive myself. Then, with confidence that my wrong has been stricken from my record, I get back up; brush myself off; make amends, if necessary; and, with renewed resolve, step right back onto the playing field, where I can continue making progress and making history.

Accept-ions

To make peace with the past, we're going to have to accept some things about our hurts and hang-ups; so here are some *accept-ions*—what we need to accept about our hurt and anger that will help us beat our blowups! Start with this one-size-fits-all declaration "I accept it—I've fallen and I can get back up, but I will [B]etter." Then we can...

+ Accept that anger is a part of life and is a fleeting emotion, not a way of life.

+ Accept that we cannot control other people's behavior.

+ Accept that even though we may get angry, we can't keep avoiding issues.

+ Accept that we do not have to view every conflict as a personal attack.

+ Accept that we do not have to overcompensate to atone for our anger. A sincere apology should suffice.

+ Accept that my-way-or-no-way thinking will only keep us living angry.

+ Accept that unresolved anger can kill us quickly or slowly. For example, we can either experience blowups, rising blood pressure, or a sudden heart attack; or depression, isolation, or a chronic disease.

+ Accept that unresolved anger can kill others, as in instances of blind rage, crimes of passion, and mass murders.

+ Accept that hatred is unacceptable, including hatred of ourselves and others.

+ Accept the need in most instances for a cooling-off period.

+ Accept the need to avoid brooding and instead develop coping strategies and alternate solutions. (Starting with better-life builders.)

+ Accept that all stormy seas will eventually calm. Meaning, this too shall pass. I can, and will overcome. Starting now.

BUILDERS AND BLOCKERS: RESENTMENT VERSUS AFFECTION

If we allow hurt or anger about an injustice to age for too long, it will eventually ferment into the better-life blocker universally known as *resentment*.

Resentment

Resentment is "the feeling of displeasure or indignation at some act, remark, person, etc., regarded as causing injury or insult."[16]

To discover whether or not resentment is clogging up your progress, consider this brief definition and what it looks and acts like when it burns inside someone. Which of the following characteristics do you see in yourself?

---

16. "resentment," *Dictionary.com*, http://www.dictionary.com/browse/resentment?s=t .

How Resentment Looks and Acts

A resentful person is antagonistic, begrudging, bitter, defensive, indignant, offended, spiteful, negative, cynical, and harbors hard feelings. This person has an overbearing attitude and may feel entitled to certain things. They may act as if they have a chip on their shoulder. They carry excessive grief and ill will toward specific people and incidents. They actively try to justify their grudges and look for chances to describe in great detail what has happened to them. They may display aggressive and destructive behavior toward self, others, or property. A person with resentment tends to overreact, losing their temper and becoming verbally abusive. They may act depressed to appear passive and to elicit pity, but they refuse to be comforted. They tend to withdraw or isolate themselves, and may drastically alter eating and sleeping habits. Suppressed hostility often surfaces in resistance to or rebellion against authority.

Make It Personal

Resist the urge to think about someone else this may apply to. Be honest—this is about you. List any ways you see resentment evident in your present behavior.

Forgiveness

Making peace with the past almost always requires the better-life builder of *forgiveness*, whether for ourselves or for others. To *forgive* means "to grant pardon for…an offense,…to give up all claim on account of; to grant pardon to (a person); to cease to feel resentment against; to cancel an indebtedness."[17] To help you better understand forgiveness, study this definition and the following description of how forgiveness looks and acts. Which of the following characteristics would you like to incorporate into your life?

---

17. "forgive," *Dictionary.com*, http://www.dictionary.com/browse/forgive?s=t.

How Forgiveness Looks and Acts

A forgiving person bears with others, turns the other cheek, wipes the slate clean, accepts apologies, and lets go of the past. They know that forgiving and letting go are not dependent upon an apology or an admission of guilt. They understand that holding on to grudges can lead to physical, mental, spiritual, relational, and financial damage. They realize that feeling "forgiving" is not necessary to willfully absolve a fault. They are willing to overlook an offense, forget about it, and to carry on as if it never happened. They are aware of their own need for mercy and are determined to offer it to others.

Forgiveness Building Material

Below are some truths about forgiveness. Take time daily to build your better life by thinking, praying, and/or saying,

> Our Father which art in heaven, hallowed be thy name. Thy kingdom come, thy will be done in earth, as it is in heaven. Give us this day our daily bread. And forgive us our debts, as we forgive our debtors....
> (Matthew 6:9–12 KJV)

> For if you forgive other people when they sin against you, your heavenly Father will also forgive you. But if you do not forgive others their sins, your Father will not forgive your sins. (Matthew 6:14–15 NIV)

"Forgotten is forgiven."
—F. Scott Fitzgerald, *The Crack-Up*

Make It Personal

Before moving on, take some time to practice the "3-R's" by asking yourself the following questions and applying them to your life.

Reflect

1. What stood out to me most in what I just read?

2. Do people think I'm cold, aloof, or arrogant?

3. If someone makes me angry, do I avoid admitting it?

4. To avoid conflict, do I ever hold in my feelings rather than stand up for myself?

5. Am I uncomfortable expressing my love for my family and friends?

6. Do I pride myself on hiding my anger?

Release

If there is anything you need to let go of, repeat the following: "After reflecting, I see that I need to let go of _____, and I choose to release it now." Humble yourself, and give all your worries and cares to God.

> *So humble yourselves under the mighty power of God, and at the right time he will lift you up in honor. Give all your worries and cares to God, for he cares about you.* (1 Peter 5:6–7)

Renew

After releasing that weight, what are some positive things you can commit to in the future?

> *Our Father which art in heaven, hallowed be thy name. Thy kingdom come, thy will be done in earth, as it is in heaven. Give us this day our daily bread. And forgive us our debts, as we forgive our debtors.* (Matthew 6:9–12 KJV)

PART 6

MAKING HISTORY:
I'M STARTING TO GET OVER MY PAST, SO WHAT NOW?

11

HISTORY LESSONS

When I was in grade school, some teachers would regularly write names on the chalkboard in an attempt to maintain order in the classroom. If anyone acted up during class, the teacher would race to the front of the room and quickly spell out his or her name in a somewhat controlled but slightly frazzled manner, a flurry of chalk loudly smacking the board with each new letter. And the name was displayed there for the rest of the day, sometimes for the whole week, and all the classes that used that room would see those names. If your name was on the board, you would receive some sort of extra disciplinary action like restricted privileges, additional homework, or hours of detention.

Teachers intentionally kept the names on the board as part of the punishment, knowing that these students would hear about it from their peers and get teased or possibly shamed. Whenever I disobeyed, I could easily accept the disciplinary action, but I really wanted my name erased from that board as soon as possible. Some kids wore it like a badge of honor, but others, like me, found it a pretty sufficient deterrent. I was very uncomfortable with somebody else pointing out what I had done. I was already down on myself for it and regretfully aware of the consequences of my actions.

History suggests that King David may have thought the same way when he was entangled in a potentially career-ending scandal that could have been just as easily pulled from today's gossip headlines: "David Caught in Adulterous Affair!" "Mistress Pregnant with King's Baby!" "Husband Murdered by King's Order!" He was so distraught that he pleaded with God not only to erase what he had done but also to renew his entire being. He cried, "*Create in me a clean heart, O God; and renew a right spirit within me*" (Psalm 51:10 KJV).

A distinct advantage in pursuing a better life with the same God that David prayed to is that He's not interested in shaming us. Throughout Scripture, God makes it clear that He does not expect us to keep compiling our own (or anybody else's) disgraces in some attempt to compensate for what we have or haven't done. He lets us take our place in grace, instead. After a wrong, we are invited to acknowledge it and then confess and release it to Him, so we don't have to sacrifice any further enjoyment of life. Repentance? Yes. Retribution? No.

Good Graces

A few years back, I walked through the halls of the county courthouse on my appointed court date. I passed police officers in uniform, prisoners in orange jumpsuits, lawyers in super sharp suits, and other people dressed in everyday clothes like me. As diverse as the people milling around were, I was sure that their stories were even more diverse, from first-time infractions and petty offenses to repeated misdemeanors and felonies. Some probably had very convincing arguments about why they shouldn't be there; but others, like me, knew they were guilty.

The courthouse itself was intimidating, the atmosphere clouded with confusion. Then to be seated inside the courtroom, feeling uneasy, and suddenly hear "All rise!" as the judge entered made it an even more formidable experience for me. I was so grateful to have my veteran police-officer friend accompany me throughout the process. I welcomed his valuable companionship and guidance in navigating the system. His long-standing relationship with the court proved to be priceless, as the pending charges of my speeding citation and driving without my license on my person were dismissed. Without him, no doubt I would have been convicted and had to spend a lot of extra time and money, only to have ended up with a tarnished record.

After coming out of that experience completely unblemished, I couldn't help but think of the verse I've heard since I was a kid in Sunday school: *"But if anyone does sin, we have an advocate who pleads our case before the Father. He is Jesus Christ, the one who is truly righteous"* (1 John 2:1). After that experience, I developed a new appreciation for what Jesus does on our behalf every single time we ask.

The simple fact of the matter is that I deserved to be convicted of those accusations. They were true—I was speeding, and I did not have my driver's license on me. But because my friend was willing to vouch for me and speak to the judge on my behalf, I was in his good graces and was absolved of all charges.

Another simple fact is that as we attempt to [B]etter today to leave a legacy of better life tomorrow, at times our screw-ups are so glaring and appear only to be getting worse. But even when we feel like a hopeless case, deserving to be prosecuted to the fullest extent of the law, if we offer a simple, heartfelt plea, in His mercy, our Defender offers grace to us by silencing all accusations and declaring us not guilty and free to go.

The grace of God is a freestanding offer to erase our name from the chalkboard, so to speak, no matter how many times it has been written there. It's a move that consistently empowers us with new opportunities simply because we accept His offer to absolve our guilt. It is that same grace that gave us the opportunity for salvation in the first place. What hinders so many of us from making peace with our past is getting all legalistic and judgmental about grace after we've accepted it. It's ludicrous for us to start trying to earn something we already have and never paid for in the first place. Keeping a long list of our and others' disgraces to prove that we are worthy of a better life only keeps up a perpetual cycle of pain and low-level living. Nowhere has Jesus ever told us to judge. He said the exact opposite: *"Do not judge, or you too will be judged"* (Matthew 7:1 NIV). The high and mighty position of a judge of everybody's behavior is not fit for a human.

Instead, we were given the free gift of grace; we should accept it as our own and give it away to others.

WHAT HINDERS SO MANY OF US FROM MAKING PEACE WITH OUR PAST IS GETTING ALL LEGALISTIC AND JUDGMENTAL ABOUT GRACE AFTER WE'VE ACCEPTED IT. IT'S LUDICROUS FOR US TO START TRYING TO EARN SOMETHING WE ALREADY HAVE AND NEVER PAID FOR IN THE FIRST PLACE.

How do you recognize if you're being legalistic? If you are harsh or hard on people, pointing out their faults and failures; or if you've been called a killjoy once or twice, you might be legalistic. Also, if you're hard on yourself and a stickler for the rules in your own life, you're almost certainly going to be hard on others and overdue to cut them some slack.

Well, then, how do you know you're being gracious? A distinct feeling of liberty marks those who are gracious. They are pleasant to be around and have a freedom of self-expression. Gracious people are merciful people—they accept others and are easy on them. They do not take themselves too seriously. Grace is a gift, and when we accept it, it positively affects how we think, feel, and act—even when things do not go according to plan.

Redo

Every one of us has had the painful misfortune of our lives not going as planned. When something goes wrong, if a teacher writes our name on the chalkboard or we end up in the courthouse, it is completely natural to feel down about the undesired turn of events for a while. But as you and I continue moving forward, we can't allow that frustration to linger too long; we need to put time limits on our gloominess. Then, as that time expires, we simply must exercise our minds over the matter, stop feeling sad or sorry for ourselves, and look for lessons we can take away from the experience.

I remember listening to a football coach talk about the differences be-tween winning and losing, explaining how he didn't really learn too much from the wins, but he could write a book on the lessons he learned from the losses. One of those lessons could be developing a short attention span when it comes to fault and failure. Tough circumstances present us with the opportunity for growth by showing us sides of ourselves we didn't even know we had—valuable gems of character that might never have been un-covered any other way except by going through a hellish loss. We have the power to decide to ditch the despair and, as the old song goes, "put on a happy face." When we look to God for strength to overcome the pain of our past, we will discover that our stamina increases, our stories be-come more interesting, and our stress management starts inspiring others. Turning our focus toward the God who specializes in turning weaknesses into strengths provides the ultimate demonstration that we can gain a win from a loss.

WHEN WE LOOK TO GOD FOR STRENGTH TO OVERCOME THE PAIN OF OUR PAST, WE WILL DISCOVER THAT OUR STAMINA INCREASES, OUR STORIES BECOME MORE INTERESTING, AND OUR STRESS MANAGEMENT STARTS INSPIRING OTHERS.

A few times in grade school, our entire class would do so poorly on a test that our teacher, fortunately, would have mercy on us all, throw out the results, and announce a redo. And of course, after reviewing the old tests, we had an opportunity to drastically improve our performance the next time around.

It has been said in so many different ways that failure produces inven-tion and that repetition is the mother of skill. If both of those sayings are true, then failure, or learning things the hard way, time after time, ought to result in some incredible inventions and skills. If we're perceptive while traveling on the road to better things, we will likely start to look at failure in a different light. It's possible for us, and preferable to those within ear-shot, to stop complaining about our losses and challenges and start appreciating them for what they could be—life lessons.

Okay, so maybe you've learned only what *not* to do; that's still a valuable part of any education. Once you're painfully aware that taking a certain path always leads to frustration, you'll likely choose another path, or make adjustments to avoid the same outcome. Painful experiences led auto-industry pioneer Henry Ford to utter his well-known statement, "Failure is simply the opportunity to begin again, this time more intelligently." Less-than-stellar results were also behind inventor Thomas Edison's confession, "I have not failed. I've just found ten thousand ways that won't work." And again, one of my favorite sports figures of all time, Michael Jordan, summed up his past simply and honestly when he said, "I've failed over and over and over again in my life and that is why I succeed."

Education is valuable and necessary, but alongside formal instruction, there is life experience, which can be gained only by living it. As time passes and our perspectives change, we realize that falling down produces the knowledge, skills, and strategies necessary to get back up and keep climbing upward. It requires gumption to follow that timeless admonition we all learned as kids, probably sometime during grade school, "If at first you don't succeed, try, try, try again."

Practice

"Trying again" is also known as practice. Oh, how I used to hate it when I saw that word on my list of chores when I was a kid! Somewhere on the list, in between my other weekly duties—mow the lawn, vacuum, sweep the garage, feed the horses, clean the stalls—was the word *practice*. That meant I was supposed to practice playing the piano for thirty minutes. While I didn't necessarily *love* the other chores I had to do (I mean, I don't imagine anyone would actually love shoveling horse manure), I didn't hate them, either; but for some reason, I absolutely loathed practicing the piano. I just wanted to go outside and play with my friends. I begged my parents to let me quit. They said, "When you get older, you'll really wish you hadn't quit." At that age, I didn't care, so I kept begging. I guess they must have gotten sick of my whining about it, because they finally let me quit. Guess what? They were right. I really wish I didn't quit.

However, because it was during the initial craze over the movie, the one piece of music I did like to play over and over during those years was the *Star Wars* theme song. And do you know the one piece of music I still know how to play to this day? You guessed it! How did that happen? Practice. I don't even have to think about playing that song. It's so etched in my memory that I can sit down at any keyboard anywhere at any time and plink out the best one-fingered version of the *Star Wars* theme song you've ever heard!

We act certain ways without thinking, because we have repeated those actions enough times to make them automatic. It's a simple equation: Practice + practice + practice = habit. If our hurtful actions have become thoughtless habits, then we must retrain our brains.

How do we do that? Well, you know how studying or rehearsing something over and over again usually helps us to learn it? That's really the simplest way to train our brain. We can trace the process back thousands of years, at least to Psalm 1, where even before becoming king, David gave us his take on the best training regimen to follow: *"Blessed is the man who walks not in the counsel of the wicked…but his delight is in the law of the LORD, and on his law he meditates day and night.… In all that he does, he prospers"* (Psalm 1:1–3 ESV).

Meditate means to contemplate. In the original Hebrew, it means "to mutter,"[18] or to repeat, and when we follow David's advice, meditating on good things, success shows up. So in the same way we learn to ride a bike or play the piano, we can learn God's Word. When we read, reread, dream about, and speak good things out loud, especially God's Word, our minds will be remolded. When we think better, we'll act better. We will literally begin to form new pathways in our brains, allowing us to cross over troubled waters and walk into new territory. Whenever we start to think we're stuck in an old habit or frame of mind, we need to think again. We need to think better of ourselves, and then think again. And again…practice can perfect.

---

18. "meditate," *Strong's Exhaustive Concordance*, http://biblehub.com/hebrew/1897.htm.

Forget It

We have to understand that the biggest threat to living a new life is our old life. The most powerful enemy of our future is our past. However, our past can also be one of our biggest allies. It depends on what we do with it.

Second Corinthians 5:17 (KJV) says, "*Therefore if any man be in Christ, he is a new creature: old things are passed away; behold, all things are become new.*" Our decision to be in Christ changes our position. In the same vein, another Scripture gives more of a directive about how to operate in the new position: "*Forget the former things; do not dwell on the past. See, I am doing a new thing! Now it springs up; do you not perceive it? I am making a way in the wilderness and streams in the wasteland*" (Isaiah 43:18–19 NIV). That lets us know there's more to life than our past has shown us. No matter what the wilderness looked like, or how much time we feel like we have wasted there, if we will intentionally forget it, there is the promise of something new!

You might say, "But I can't forget. I tried, and it hasn't worked." There is good news for you. Did you know you can *learn* to forget? It's true. I know it may be hard to believe because so many of us have rehearsed negative memories or habits far too long, even though they produce nothing but pain.

The temptation is to keep up the thinking patterns we learned from reality TV or inherited from the family tree: *This is the way we've always dealt with things. Well, we don't actually deal with things, we just talk about how bad things have gotten. Then we pull others into our drama.* But those kinds of negative rehearsals eventually become resentments. It is like drinking poison and expecting the ones who hurt us to die. Instead of rehearsing our regrets so often that we feel like we can't forget, why don't we practice forgetting, instead? All it requires is turning our attention elsewhere. At one time or other, some of us may have said (or thought), "Oh, I'll forgive, but I'll never forget." If this is you, start now by renouncing that vow, then release it to God and renew your commitment to live better by forgetting along with forgiving. How do you learn to do that? Practice.

Just about everywhere we look, we can see either chaos or calmness. It does not matter whether we are at home, at school, or on the job, our disposition depends on where we choose to concentrate our attention. If one person says, "Everywhere I look, I see so much chaos, pain, and hopelessness," and another person says, "Everywhere I look, I see so much peace, beauty, and love," who is right? Actually, they both are right. The object of their focus is reflected in their outlook. Sometimes, all we need to do to change our outlook is to change our intake. If everything has been bad lately, and you don't like what you're seeing, it may be time to look at something else. We can literally change our lives simply by changing our minds. The Bible says that we can rid our mind of wrong thinking and make it think on what is right. (See 2 Corinthians 10:5.) We just have to practice doing it—forgetting the bad and switching our attention to the good.

WE CAN LITERALLY CHANGE OUR LIVES SIMPLY BY CHANGING OUR MINDS.

Some may argue, "Well, I'm not going to stick my head in the sand and act oblivious to what has happened to me, or what's going on around me now." I agree wholeheartedly. We don't have to pretend that we live in a perfect world. We need to be aware of what has happened and is happening, even if it's horrible; but that doesn't mean we have to dwell on it and make it the center of our universe. It's like changing the channel on our television—we are aware of what's on certain channels, but we decide to watch something else. We can do the same in our brain.

I've been inspired so many different times by a simple little story I heard about a woman my parents spent some time with during the 1970s. Kathryn Kuhlman was a famous healing evangelist who endured bouts of negative publicity due to her prominence during a time when society was not yet very accepting of women in such roles. She had to develop thicker skin and, likely, practice forgetting. Occasionally, she would encounter some of the people who had written or said awful things about her, and Ms. Kuhlman's aide would ask her how she wanted to handle it. Kathryn's reply was one that I have been repeatedly challenged by and found inspirational. In her sweet demeanor, she would whisper something like, "Oh, honey, we're just going to pretend like that never happened."

To leave the past behind and enjoy the present, we need to practice forgetting our unpleasantries and break our addiction to drama. Then we can start taking the advice of the old Monty Python tune, "Always Look on the Bright Side of Life."

12

LONG TIME COMING

W hen you don't know what to do, don't do anything." Through the years, I have found this word of advice from a wise family friend incredibly valuable. When facing a decision with no clear direction about which way to go, I wait before just plowing ahead. Unfortunately, I've also had to learn that truth the hard way more than a few times; I've realized that when we move too quickly, we often create a crisis that could have been avoided if we would have just waited awhile.

Similar to my friend's counsel, most of us have been offered the true albeit fortune-cookie type of wisdom that advises, "Time is the wisest counselor." We simply shouldn't rush things. Rushed jobs are usually not done well. As cliché as it may sound, this basic truth applies to learning to live a better life; it is an ongoing process that requires patience. Of course, by now we know that nothing happens overnight. Throughout this book and "The Better Life Course," our systematic efforts are directed toward making peace with the past so we can start enjoying the present. As we learn to embrace our moments, we can start designing our future and learning how to live our dreams.

The Waiting Game

The shepherd boy David who became king and weathered the storms of scandal knew all about the waiting game, but he wrote about what happens when we look to God for direction:

I waited patiently for the LORD to help me, and he turned to me and heard my cry. He lifted me out of the pit of despair, out of the mud and the mire. He set my feet on solid ground and steadied me as I walked along. He has given me a new song to sing, a hymn of praise to our God. Many will see what he has done and be amazed. They will put their trust in the LORD.   (Psalm 40:1–3)

Are you like me or like David? In this excursion of recovering what we've lost and discovering who we really are, do we need regular reminders to be patient? One valuable piece of information about patience comes from David's son Solomon, who wrote in Proverbs 16:32 (NIV), *"Better a patient person than a warrior, one with self-control than one who takes a city."* And again in Proverbs 19:2, *"Enthusiasm without knowledge is no good; haste makes mistakes."* Even though a calm, even-tempered person may receive a lot less fanfare than a rash, wild warrior, he is often more reliable and experiences better results.

So many things in our day-to-day lives take longer than we think they should. As I've mentioned before, I often feel myself losing my cool or starting to compile a complaint. This, of course, accomplishes nothing, except making me and anyone else around me upset. At that point, sometimes I recall from my childhood one of my mom's frequent admonitions to be patient, only now God is the One gently reminding me that patience is truly a virtue. What we have to keep in mind as we build a better life is that God's plan for us is so intricate and perfect that it takes some time for all the pieces to be put into place. Scripture says, *"But let patience have her perfect work, that ye may be perfect and entire, wanting nothing"* (James 1:4 KJV).

Can you imagine what it would be like to be perfectly complete and wanting for absolutely nothing? The way I understand the verse, the more patient we are, the more content and satisfied we are. "Life is short," people say. But sometimes, life feels incredibly long. So by exercising patience more and more, we'll find ourselves enjoying more stages of life with a peaceful state of mind.

WHAT WE HAVE TO KEEP IN MIND AS
WE BUILD A BETTER LIFE IS THAT GOD'S PLAN
FOR US IS SO INTRICATE AND PERFECT
THAT IT TAKES SOME TIME FOR ALL THE PIECES
TO BE PUT INTO PLACE.

No matter what we're waiting on, remember, it's nothing to get anxious about. Anxiousness turns into frustration, forcing us down a slippery slope of dark thoughts and emotional angst. Adding to that futility is the danger of those pent-up feelings turning venomous, leading to relational, mental, and physical breakdowns. It's just not worth it to get all worked up over snail-paced situations, whether it be traffic, a slow waiter, a long-overdue promotion, loved ones pushing our buttons, or the dragging tempo of our progression. Yes, we all want to feel better and healthy, and to sense that life is moving forward. That's why the sense of calmness that patience brings to our mind, body, and behavior is such a priceless attribute. Not only will it lengthen our life span, it will improve the quality of *every* experience—the good, the bad, and even the big, long, horribly ugly ones. Our best bet is to remember that the longer the wait, the sweeter the reward.

Nothing to Fear

We know that it takes time to grieve, heal, and grow after all the monkey wrenches have been thrown into the middle of our lives, especially ones thrown by people we have trusted deeply. When that happens, undoubtedly our hearts ache; we may shed some tears and feel a bit numb and wonder, *Why me?* But whatever the reason, which may never be uncovered, after feeling sorry for ourselves has reached its maximum amount of allotted time, we have a decision to make. As trite as it may sound, it really does boil down to deciding whether to be bitter or [B]etter. We have to honestly ask ourselves if we want to spend all our energy staying angry and planning our revenge, or if we want to grow from the trouble, making it into our own personal school of hard knocks.

After the initial period of shock, pain, and numbness caused by the "not in love with you anymore" statement from my wife, I felt myself growing extremely angry, and it showed up in all kinds of ways. For a little while, I was okay with the feeling. In my mind, I was arguably justified in my craving to lash out to hurt someone like I had been hurt. Right after I had started feeling that way, however, I came across one of God's promises in Isaiah 41. As I read verse 10, I froze. It felt like it arrested me right as I sat there at my desk. So then I read it out loud (you might want to read it out loud for yourself, too), and it sounded like this:

> *Fear not [there is nothing to fear], for I am with you; do not look around you in terror and be dismayed, for I am your God. I will strengthen and harden you to difficulties, yes, I will help you; yes, I will hold you up and retain you with My [victorious] right hand of rightness and justice.* (Isaiah 41:10 AMPC)

Right then, it clicked as a moment of truth, causing me to recognize how futile my puny attempts at evening the score would turn out. They would only aggravate things, not alleviate them. Besides, I had just grasped God's promise that He would strengthen and harden my heart so attacks wouldn't hurt so much. It was the beginning of my line of thinking, *If I can take this, I can take anything.*

No matter the tumultuous times of your past, the fact is, you made it through! You're still here, so now is the time to redeem what was wrong. Think about Joseph's story, which was made into a Broadway production called *Joseph and the Amazing Technicolor Dreamcoat*. After all he had been through—beat up by his brothers, thrown into a pit, left for dead, sold into slavery, lied about, put into prison—he became the second most powerful man in all the land! During that long process, I'm sure there were plenty of times his patience wore thin; but he held on to his dream through it all! Perhaps, looking back at all that had happened, he recognized the value in every part of it. Yes, hindsight truly is 20/20. He said to the very same brothers who betrayed him, *"You intended to harm me, but God intended it all for good. He brought me to this position so I could save the lives of many people"* (Genesis 50:20).

I wonder how many people will be affected by *your* willingness to reconstruct your thoughts about the past. If you allow God to alter how you see your hurt, you may actually become all you were meant to be, and have a huge impact on others. Your story may not ever be turned into a Broadway production like Joseph's, but by making a few adjustments to your mentality and motivation, you can enhance your story and make it appeal to a much wider audience.

Power Moves

It's true that we should wait a while if we don't know what to do, and that a "while" is different for everyone and every situation. But sometimes, we keep our audience waiting too long. Some traumatic chapters drag on so long that we feel justified in waiting for them to work themselves out, but there always comes a time when we have to make some moves.

This reminds me of a hairstylist who told me, "I've been working weekends since 1995," just as she finished cutting my hair.

As I got up out of the chair, I asked, "Oh, so that's the schedule you like best?"

"No," she said, "I hate it, but what can you do about it?"

I didn't have the chance to say anything then, but as I walked away, I thought, *What can you do about something you hate?* Now, I don't have all the answers, but in her case and in ours, I do have an idea worth considering: make a move! This hairstylist had been on a schedule she loathed for twenty years because she had yet to tap into the greatest agent of change she would ever encounter in her lifetime—herself!

If you have a job that grates on your nerves, or you can't stand your schedule, or you're in a relationship that's lost its luster, or anything else that is going against the grain of who you are, what should you do? If you sit back and wait for the winds of change to blow, or the sun to finally shine, or that ship to come in, you're going to be waiting a long time. Waiting for others to somehow magically feel our pain so that they move heaven and earth to put us where we need to be is like holding on to a broken compass. It will get us nowhere. All my life, I've heard folks say that they're just waiting on God to do something for them. God works on behalf of those who wait on Him, but we have an active part to play in the process. We can't just sit around complaining about the lack of movement if we aren't making any moves.

GOD WORKS ON BEHALF OF THOSE WHO WAIT ON HIM, BUT WE HAVE AN ACTIVE PART TO PLAY IN THE PROCESS. WE CAN'T JUST SIT AROUND COMPLAINING ABOUT THE LACK OF MOVEMENT IF WE AREN'T MAKING ANY MOVES.

There's so much truth in the old saying that God helps those who help themselves that it has often been mistakenly attributed to the Bible. But Scripture is full of directives that we have a power greater than ourselves inside of us. He who is in us "*is able to do immeasurably more than all we ask or imagine, according to his power that is at work within us*" (Ephesians 3:20 NIV). Confidence is knowing that "*greater is he that is in* [us]" (1 John 4:4 KJV), and that "[we] *can do all things through Christ who strengthens* [us]" (Philippians 4:13 NKJV). We are *able* even when we feel *disabled*.

If you're dissatisfied, if you want more, if you feel stirred up, there's a reason. Your heart's desires are not there to frustrate you but to motivate you to actively fulfill them. But don't wait for others to make all the moves—you move what you can to get into better position!

How should we respond when we hear things like, "Oh, no, he's back in jail," "You're being laid off," or "Your account is overdrawn"? I know nobody wants to get that call that sends his world into upheaval. It may be about a rebellious child, a disappearing job, or a lack of money, or perhaps it is the small trials that wear on us over time, such as the antics of our spouse, or the sum total of all of them, and more. Dealing with crises is not anybody's favorite way to spend the days, months, and years. But crises visit us all.

The components of each crisis may vary for everyone, but one characteristic is constant: potential power.

Power? Yes. Power. Hear me out on this. Within every crisis lies the possibility of reinvention. When something goes wrong, it reveals our true selves—perhaps we need an adjustment or realignment or just a fresh perspective. Otherwise, the whole hot potato wouldn't have landed in our lap in the first place, right? That's the thing about crisis; it gets our attention, at least for a little while. But then what?

We have two choices. We can work to change and improve the situation, or we can ignore it and just learn to live with it. The problem with ignoring it is that, when another dilemma comes along and demands our attention, we may start to feel truly overwhelmed. Often, when too many hot button issues culminate at one time, it ends badly.

"But it seems as if I'm just making it worse by getting into it. It just stirs stuff up when I address it." I know. It does. But maybe it will slowly start heading in the right direction, or maybe it will stay unresolved. That's usually because other people's wills and attitudes and issues are involved. But at the very least, you will have the peace of mind that you took responsibility, faced the situation head on, and gave it your best shot. You can rest easy knowing that you've done all you know what to do up to this point. And who knows? Maybe there will be a break in the action. Maybe you'll get another idea to try or another chance to act. Sometimes, though, you will just have to mark it down as "You win some, you lose some."

Just know that at the end of any crisis, whether resolved or unresolved, you will have won because you made moves and grew stronger. You went face-to-face with the beast of an issue, and it didn't kill you—it brought something better out of you. It brought you power! You will have a new experience and, more than likely, a greater boldness to handle new things.

The Sweet Sixteen

So to interrupt unwanted patterns, we know we have to do as much as we can with what is inside us and what is offered to us, but we don't have to do everything all at once. That would be a terrible idea, and it would probably backfire, making things worse than they were before. But if we truly want to [B]etter ourselves, our family, and our future, we have to do *something* about it. To break out of old practices, we need some new ones. Now, because I'm a huge fan of transforming ideas into practical steps, I made a list of new habits to replace our old habits. Here are my sweet sixteen suggestions.

1. Make Like Magic

For a time, disappear from all people, surroundings, and circumstances that contribute to unwanted behavior. Think about it, if you could get away from all your commiserating companions (the ones with whom you sit around talking about how "it's not fair") and clear your head, you'd probably develop a new perspective.

2. Recruit a Healing Helper

Just as every kid performs better in sports or school programs if someone is there to watch him, so everybody needs somebody to lean on. Having a close, trustworthy person who believes in you and encourages you will empower you to [B]etter and make peace with your past and anything else that comes up in your future.

3. Check Your Mirrors

Regularly reflect (you can use the "3-R's") on where you are right now. We will never get where we want to be if we don't get real about where we are now. Only you truly know you. Be honest with yourself about how you're doing and adjust accordingly.

4. Reassign Past Pain

Don't allow the past to discourage you; instead, let it encourage you. Consider how far you've come and what you've learned. You may not have made it to where you want to be, but every once in a while, glance back at where you used to be, so you can see your progress!

5. Read! Read! Read!

Find books on subjects that interest you and read for knowledge as well as just for fun. Remember, leaders are readers. If you believe you're going to be leading, you had better start reading!

6. Keep On Keepin' On

There are no magic cures for making old habits disappear overnight. Life is an endurance sport, but the prizes are worth the pain. Maybe you used to be a quitter; if so, it's time to turn over a new leaf. There's no substitution for that good, old-fashioned, four-letter word, *work!* The accumulation of work is a powerful thing.

7. Reject Rejection's Suggestions

Reject the thoughts of unworthiness and ugliness, and replace them with quality memories, experiences, and relationships. Don't dwell on thoughts like, *I'm not worth much; No one could love me;* or *I'll never be happy.* Instead, set your mind on the truths of Scripture: *"I am fearfully and wonderfully made"* (Psalm 139:14 NIV); *"I can do all things through Christ"* (Philippians 4:13 KJV); *"With God all things are possible"* (Matthew 19:26 KJV).

8. Don't Be a Dweller

The mind can entertain a very limited number of thoughts at a time—exactly one! So contemplate the progress in your life. Don't dwell on the past, because you need to be prepared to handle new things in the future.

9. Respond, Don't React

Practice keeping your spirit in the right spot—on top and in control of your body, mind, will, and emotions. For situations you know you'll encounter, plan your responses ahead of time so you're prepared. Consistency is key in strengthening the foundation for a bright future.

10. Act As If

Keep in mind that you are a one-of-a-kind work of art, so act as if you are valuable. Take good care of your spirit, mind, and body. Carry yourself with confidence and expect goodness to follow you. Don't forget that your body is a temple, and you need to treat it as such.

11. Reach Out

To help yourself, help others. When you invest your time, talent, energy, and/or finances in a cause, you'll get better in a hurry. Find something you can take on as a personal project, and make it your mission to see it improve.

12. Get Grateful

Deciding to be thankful for what you have will take you off "victim island" and put you back into reality, allowing you to see how good you have it. Never forget there are always people who don't have it as good as you. Getting grateful releases mood-improving chemicals into the bloodstream; gratitude always improves the attitude.

13. Have a Hobby

All work and no play definitely makes you dull. When you do something just for the fun of it, it does a lot for you. Hobbies help you redirect your mind away from somber issues, stimulate creativity, acquire new knowledge, and form new relationships with people who have similar interests.

14. Pursue Passion

By practicing the daily disciplines of prayer, meditation, and Bible study, and spending quality time with like-minded people, your passion will present itself. The more you pursue connection with your Creator, the more He'll reveal to you why you were created. You will start to see His direction for your life through everyday conversations, circumstances, and common sense.

15. Smile

Notify your facial muscles that you have decided to be a shiny, contagious example of what God can do with a person dedicated to living a better life. You know the saying "Smile, and the world smiles with you;"[19] so let's see those pearly whites!

16. Laugh

A lot. Doctors say that a hearty laugh massages the inner organs, and the Bible says that laughter is like medicine. (See Proverbs 17:22.) So laugh hard to live long. Go ahead and try it right now!

Just like we talked about in chapter 1, "For Better," a little bit can go a long way. So try one or two of these suggestions at a time, and, over time, try them all as you make peace with the past on the way to your better life.

---

19. Stanley Gordon West, *Growing an Inch* (Minneapolis, MN: Lexington-Marshall Publishing, 2003).

BUILDERS AND BLOCKERS:
ADDICTION VERSUS DEVOTION

If any of our unhealthy habits appear to be uncontrollable, most likely we are dealing with a better-life blocker of *addiction*.

Addiction

Addiction is "the state of being enslaved to a habit or practice or to something that is psychologically or physically habit-forming, as narcotics, to such an extent that its cessation causes severe trauma."[20] To discover whether or not addiction may be blocking you, consider this brief description and the types of behavior that characterize addiction. Which of the following do you see in yourself?

How Addiction Looks and Acts

A person with an addiction is deceptive, delusional, dependent, obsessive, reactionary, and secretive. They will make any excuse for addictive

---

20. "addiction," *Dictionary.com*, http://www.dictionary.com/browse/addiction?s=t.

behavior, and they hide behind denial, cleverly deflecting responsibility and/or blame. They may self-medicate pain or any uncomfortable feeling, and they frequently display immature behavior. They have erratic mood swings, lowered inhibitions, and blurred boundaries. This person leads a double life, may hide legal or financial problems, and is unwilling to be honest with themselves and others. They have a false sense of security or connection with others, experience chronic relationship trouble, and often prefer isolation. They regularly battle self-hatred, self-destructive thoughts, and/or suicidal tendencies.

Make It Personal

Resist the urge to think about someone else this may apply to. Be honest—this is about you. Take a moment to list any ways you see addiction evident in your present behavior.

Devotion

Making peace with the past becomes a way of life when we have the better-life builder of *devotion*. Devotion is a "profound dedication…[an] earnest attachment to a cause, person, etc.; an assignment or appropriation to any purpose."[21] To begin recognizing devotion on your journey, study this definition and the following qualities of devotion. How can you begin incorporating them into your life as you keep making history?

How Devotion Looks and Acts

A person with devotion is allegiant, committed, earnest, faithful, passionate, reverent, and sincere. They actively look for volunteer opportunities and enjoy promoting and recruiting volunteers for certain causes. They achieve a satisfactory sense of well-being when engaged in the activity or cause, and an increased sense of synergy when participating in a group. They are unwavering in their resolve to stand up for a certain cause, which produces boldness in other parts of their life. They enjoy a growing sense of

---

21. "devotion," *Dictionary.com*, http://www.dictionary.com/browse/devotion?s=t.

self-awareness of their purpose and true identity, and their ever-improving quality of life is attractive to others.

Devotion Building Material

Repetition builds skill. So take time daily to build your better life by thinking, praying, and/or saying:

I have been called to live in freedom, but I don't use it to satisfy my sinful nature. Instead, I use my freedom to serve others in love. (See Galatians 5:13.)

> "Whatever I have tried to do in life; whatever I have devoted myself to, I have devoted myself completely."
> —Charles Dickens, *David Copperfield*

Make It Personal

To what or to whom do I need to become more devoted? Before moving on, take time to practice the "3-R's" by asking yourself the following questions and applying them to your life.

Reflect

1. How does this chapter apply to my life?
2. When was the last time I rushed things and got into trouble?
3. What am I waiting on now?
4. Am I overdue for making a move?
5. Whom do I want to influence by building a better life?
6. Which sweet-sixteen habit do I need to start practicing immediately?

Release

If there is anything you need to let go of, repeat the following: "After reflecting, I see that I need to let go of _____, and I choose to release it now. Then pray this Scripture over your life:

> Create in me a clean heart, O God; and renew a right spirit within
> me.   (Psalm 51:10 KJV)

Renew

After releasing so much of your past, what are some positive things you can commit to in the future?

> Now all glory to God, who is able, through his mighty power at work
> within us, to accomplish infinitely more than we might ask or think.
>   (Ephesians 3:20)

CONCLUSION:
WHAT MATTERS MOST

After my honeymoon, I suddenly realized I had an instant family, complete with a wife and two step-cats. The relationship with the furry ones was touch and go at first, but before long, we accepted one another as friends, and I adopted them as my own. Now I love those furry little guys.

Life with cats is relatively easy, except for one thing: fur. Everywhere. Those guys shed not only during the spring but during the summer, fall, and winter, too. We find loose fur clinging to the couch, the carpet, our clothes, and other places you wouldn't believe. Patience is a must, as well as lots of lint rollers stashed around the house to keep the hair balls to a minimum.

Cats aren't alone, though. Every living thing, including dogs, horses, snakes, butterflies, and even humans shed. Our skin continuously rids itself of dead cells and is completely regenerated every twenty-eight days. Leaving behind old things is a natural part of growth and progression. The apostle Paul talked about this in Philippians 3:13 (NIV): *"One thing I do: Forgetting what is behind and straining toward what is ahead."*

Some situations, even awful ones, last for a season. Then it's time to move on. There are so many different life pursuits and activities that are both enjoyable and useful for a time; then the time comes to step out of them into something else. People known as movers and shakers routinely step away from jobs, acquaintances, accomplishments, fitness levels, and even emotional states to move onward and upward. Ultimately, all of us, like butterflies, will slip out of the shell of our bodies to move into the afterlife.

Any time is a good time to start contemplating what things may have already served their time and purpose in our lives. Including the pain of the past. There is no doubt that idea interests you, or you never would have picked up a book full of ideas for overcoming obstacles and making peace with the past. Perhaps that time has finally come, and now you have some tools to help you let go enough to go forward.

Throughout these pages, we've learned that we can counter the better-life blockers of doubt, pride, fear, rejection, resentment, and addiction with the better-life builders of belief, humility, courage, affection, forgiveness, and devotion. If we don't do this from time to time, we accumulate resistance. Then, every motion we make becomes a huge ordeal, and, after a while, we just get tired of trying and settle in one spot.

No one wants to be found settling. But it happens all too frequently. People settle in jobs they no longer enjoy or settle in dating relationships, friendships, or social groups that used to be fun but have lost their thrill. It is especially common in our emotional attachments to outdated but familiar things. These attachments are painful, damaging, and restrictive, but they're familiar, so we hold on to them.

Furthermore, too many of us fear that if we were to pick up and move on, we'd leave others behind and be labeled "selfish." So we stay, feeling like a prisoner in our own skin. Have you ever been in situations in which it felt like your skin was crawling? That may not be such a bad thing. I think it's one of God's ways of telling us that there is something better available if we will just wiggle out of the old in preparation for the new.

We need to take an inventory to see if there are any areas in our life that used to bring joy but now bring only pain, or ones that make our skin crawl and leave us feeling like we are going to have a meltdown. Those are surefire red flags waving at us—signs that it's time to lighten up and rid ourselves of that old deadweight so we can move onward and upward.

Even after learning all these helpful builders and blockers, there will still be times we are tempted with the thoughts *What's wrong with the way I am? I don't need to change. It just seems like too much work.* That's when we have to pause and realize that we're making it way too complicated. Jesus had a knack for explaining things in such simple terms, and concerning this He said, "*The work of God is this: to believe in the one he has sent*" (John 6:29 NIV).

That's pretty simple, right? He was referring to Himself, the One the Father sent to earth to actually make better life available for us. When we make getting better too much work, you and I have to remind ourselves what matters most and to decide simply to *believe* in Jesus. We all believe in something, anyway. You may say, "I don't believe in anything," but that is a belief. You might as well put your belief to work by believing in Someone instead of nothing. When we believe in Him, all things are possible. An old saying we've all probably heard from a parent or teacher at least once while growing up is, "Anything worth having is worth working for." In this case, our work to [B]etter is as easy as regularly expressing our belief *in* Jesus *to* Jesus. It provides Him with an all-access pass into every area of our lives, so that He can escort us to a better life.

ABOUT THE AUTHOR

With his inspirational influence already spanning more than twenty years, forty states, and thirty countries, Randal Smalls, "The Better Life Coach," continues to empower individuals and groups to make their lives a dream come true. As creator of "The Better Life Course," multi-level courses designed to help people break old habits and build a life they love, Randal maintains an active schedule of coaching individuals and conducting better-life events in a variety of venues, including schools, conferences, churches, and recovery centers. He is founder of The Better Life Foundation, Inc., a privately funded nonprofit organization designed to empower and equip at-risk teens and adults to build better habits and bring dreams to life through education. Randal and his wife, Adeana, live in Orange County, California. For more information about Better Life Courses, Coaching, or Foundation, visit RandalSmalls.com.